The Tao of Teams

A GUIDE TO TEAM SUCCESS

Cresencio Torres

Pfeiffer
& COMPANY

Amsterdam • Johannesburg • Oxford
San Diego • Sydney • Toronto

Editor: Mary Ann Gardner
Production Editor: Katharine Pechtimaldjian
Cover Design: Tom Lewis, Inc.
Interior Designer: Susan G. Odelson
Scribe: Mabel Lee

Library of Congress Cataloging-in-Publication Data

Torres, Cresencio, 1947-
    The Tao of teams: a guide to team success /
    Cresencio Torres.
       p.   cm.
    Includes bibliographical references.
    ISBN 0-88390-422-5
    ISBN 0-89384-258-3 (pbk.)
    1. Work groups. 2. Taoism. I. Title.
HD66.T633 1994   94-1880
658.4'036—dc20   CIP

Printed in the United States of America.

Dedication

This work is dedicated to my wife, Kathryn, my daughter, Jaimie, my grandson, Aaron, Kristen for her good reader's eye, and Laura for her editorial talent.

Contents

≡

Introduction 1

≡

Essence and the Tao of Teams 3

≡

Power and the Tao of Teams 5

≡

The Universe and the Tao of Teams 7

≡

Thinking and the Tao of Teams 9

The Eighty-one Passages of *The Tao of Teams* 13

1

Individual Empowerment 15

2

Polarity 17

3

Harmony and Growth 19

4

The Nature of Team Power 21

5

Conscience and Equity 23

6

Subtle Behavior 25

7
Acting Without Self-interest   27

8
Clarity of Values   29

9
Move Forward After Success   31

10
The Quest for Harmony and Inner Balance   33

11
Using the Team's Field   35

12
Team-Member Character   37

13
Mastering Self   39

14
Knowing the Tao   41

15
Subtle Power   43

16
Acting Natural   45

17
Leadership Is Subtle   47

18
Following the Wisdom of the Tao   49

19
Simple Actions Reflect Commitment   51

20

Seeking the Answer   53

21

The Origin of Team Power   55

22

Sharing Team Power   57

23

Attitude Is a Steady Force   59

24

Excessive Behavior   61

25

The Four Great Powers   63

26

Remaining Centered   65

27

Modeling Appropriate Behavior   67

28

Managing Forces   69

29

Noninterference   71

30

The Way to Lead   73

31

Interventions Create Discord   75

32

Maintaining an Open System   77

33
Mastery   79

34
Diversity   81

35
Creating Meaning   83

36
Team Politics   85

37
Guiding the Team   87

38
Leadership and Humility   89

39
Leadership Is Harmony   91

40
A Proven Path   93

41
Mastering the Paradox   95

42
Understanding Polarity   97

43
Subtle Use of Power   99

44
Being Successful by Needing Less   101

45
Clarity of Perception   103

46
Knowing When Enough Is Enough 105

47
Intuition Enhances One's Achievements 107

48
Pure Information Refines Instinctive Knowledge 109

49
Neutralizing Extremes Creates Balance 111

50
Recognizing the Team Cycle 113

51
A Natural and Spontaneous Path 115

52
Using the Intuitive and the Logical Mind 117

53
Unbalanced Teams Do Not Survive 119

54
Developing a Universal Perspective 121

55
Team Power Is Found in Working Together 123

56
Simplicity Contributes to Personal Power 125

57
Leading Without Interference 127

58
Micromanagement Causes a Counteraction 129

59
Moderation 131

60
Productivity 133

61
Stewardship 135

62
First Possess the Tao 137

63
A Nonconfrontational Stance 139

64
Guiding Events by Knowing Their Beginning 141

65
Subtlety Reflects One's Ability to Influence 143

66
Winning the Trust of Others 145

67
Kindness Must Be the First Virtue 147

68
Skillful Leaders 149

69
Gaining Strength by Yielding 151

70
The Tao Speaks to All 153

71
There Is Always Something That Is Unknown 155

72
Maintaining Appropriate Respect 157

73
Modeling the Tao's Natural Behavior 159

74
Restrictions Can Inhibit Development 161

75
Trust 163

76
Great Power in Flexibility 165

77
Directing the Tao's Power 167

78
Being As Yielding and Receptive As Water 169

79
Averting Lingering Resentment 171

80
Ideal Work Systems 173

81
Greater Success 175

≡

References **177**

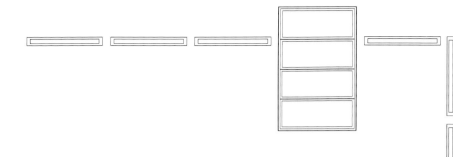

Introduction

> In my mind there must be, at the bottom of it all, not an equation, but an utterly simple idea. And to me that idea, when we finally discover it, will be so compelling, so inevitable, that we will say to one another, "Oh, how beautiful. How could it have been otherwise?"
>
> John Archibald Wheeler
> in *Leadership and the New Sciences*

The Tao of Teams is loosely taken from a translation of the ancient Chinese classic, *The Tao Te Ching,* by Lao Tzu, a gifted scholar and the custodian of the Imperial Archives twenty-six centuries ago, during the reign of the Chou Dynasty.

Tao is pronounced "dow," as in the Dow Jones Average, and is translated to mean "the way the universe works."

Te is pronounced "dir," as in the word dirt, and is translated to mean "power."

Ching is pronounced as written and is translated to mean "classic." *The Tao Te Ching* describes the all-encompassing force that operates within the universe, and it describes individual power that is derived from being in complete alignment with that force.

Similarly, *The Tao of Teams* is designed to facilitate the awareness and understanding of individual power and knowledge in relation to others, whether team members or other individuals in the organization. It explores the power that is within everyone and challenges them to create true meaning in their work. In addition, it challenges organizations to become places of learning, where the force of the Tao can be channelled into productive, high-performance endeavors.

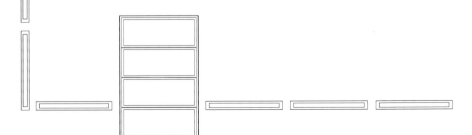

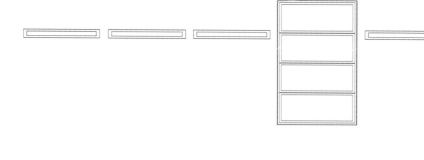

Essence and the Tao of Teams

The Tao of Teams is a dynamic collection of thoughts, sometimes paradoxical, designed to open the mind to the realities of how people form fully functioning, high-performance teams that are not often found in the workplace.

The eighty-one verses in *The Tao of Teams* challenge readers to examine their concept of team participation and encourage them to create a new meaning for their work. The essence of the Tao of team power is as follows:

≡ Know who you are as a person.

≡ Live in the world around you and understand fully your experiences.

≡ Do not depend on the opinions of others; to do so robs you of an opportunity to better understand yourself.

≡ Trust your intuition.

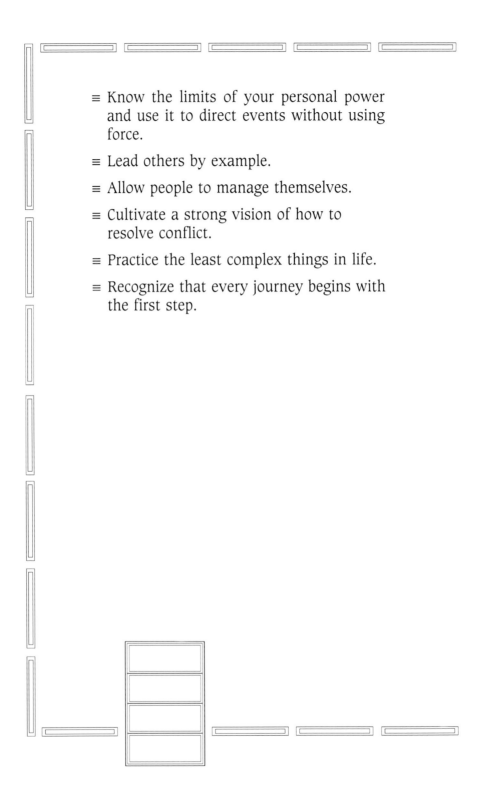

≡ Know the limits of your personal power and use it to direct events without using force.

≡ Lead others by example.

≡ Allow people to manage themselves.

≡ Cultivate a strong vision of how to resolve conflict.

≡ Practice the least complex things in life.

≡ Recognize that every journey begins with the first step.

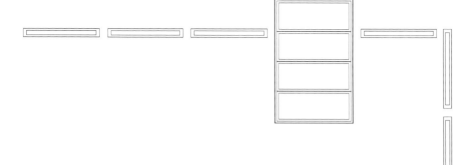

Power and the Tao of Teams

The Tao of team power penetrates the elusive notion of power possessed by each team member so that each can contribute in a synergistic fashion to the team and the organization. It allows each person to align with the forces in nature, recognizing that to be at odds with nature's way stifles creativity, learning, and growth.

An awareness of the patterns in nature can bring us insights into parallel patterns in human behavior. "Just as spring follows winter in nature, growth follows repression in society; just as too much gravity will collapse a star, too much possessiveness will collapse an idea" (Wing 1986, 12).

When team members feel powerless, they react negatively. When pushed to the extreme, they feel fear. And when they are fearful for a long time, they may feel hopeless and that all is lost. The result is that both the team and the organization fail.

On the other hand, powerful members of the team never need to show their power; yet others pay attention to them. Those who radiate the force do so with the intuitive knowledge that by allowing the force to move through them, they in turn will receive the same energy in a different form. The more they act as conductors, the more they will receive in return.

True power in team members is the ability to influence without effort. Powerful team members influence others by example and by modeling behaviors that contribute to overall team effectiveness. Within teams, powerful people have great presence. They influence those who come into contact with them by simply being present. Team members who can relate to the universal force of the Tao (the power) are actively engaged in defining and redefining their personal reality and existence. This is the force behind the Tao of team power.

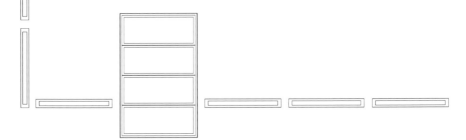

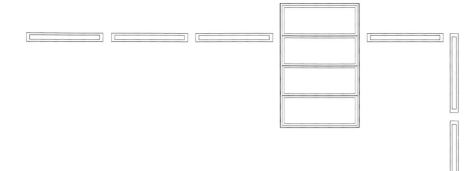

The Universe and the Tao of Teams

The Tao has been described as a unified force field that reveals a basic oneness of the universe. It has been suggested that all changes in the universe are the result of the interaction between the polar opposites: *yin* (negative) and *yang* (positive). Activity in the Tao is a continuous interplay between these forces. From this principle, we can deduce two rules for team conduct: (1) whenever you want to achieve anything, start with its opposite, and (2) when you want to keep something, include in it something of its opposite.

Change in the universe occurs not as the result of one strong force acting on something or someone else, but rather as a result of a tendency that is natural in all things and situations. Change is natural. Using force is unnatural.

Movement within the Tao is not directive; it occurs naturally and spontaneously. Since unforced activity is the Tao's principle of action, spontaneity should be a highly rewarded characteristic of all team interactions.

Fritjof Capra, in *The Tao of Physics*, suggests that acting in harmony with the universe means acting according to your values and beliefs. It means trusting your intuitive intelligence, which is innate to the human mind, just as the laws of change are innate in all things around us. If one refrains from acting contrary to nature or from going against the grain of things, one is in harmony with the Tao and, thus, one's actions will be successful.

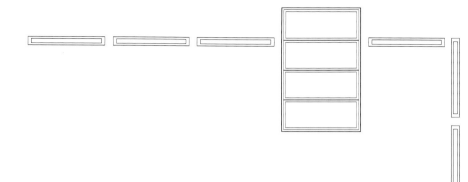

Thinking and the Tao of Teams

The Tao Te Ching was originally written in a style different from the Western literary tradition. It was written in a subjective rather than an analytical fashion, which is more common to our Western learning and reading style. *The Tao of Teams*, on the other hand, is written using both subjective and analytical approaches—right-brain and left-brain thinking processes.

Rather than approaching these verses in a sequential, linear fashion, the reader should randomly select a passage, read it, and move on to another in the same way.

By engaging both right-brain and left-brain thinking processes, we open ourselves to an understanding of *The Tao of Teams* from both a worldly and a universal perspective. We allow ourselves to examine the knowledge from an expanded awareness of our own universe.

The goal of this approach is to create a balance, or alignment, between how we feel and think, which is necessary if we are going to be working both efficiently and effectively with other people in teams. Our focus must be on the relationship (right-brain) aspects of our interactions with others rather than on the task-oriented (left-brain), impersonal side of our behavior.

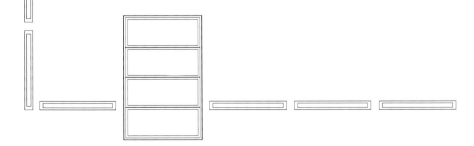

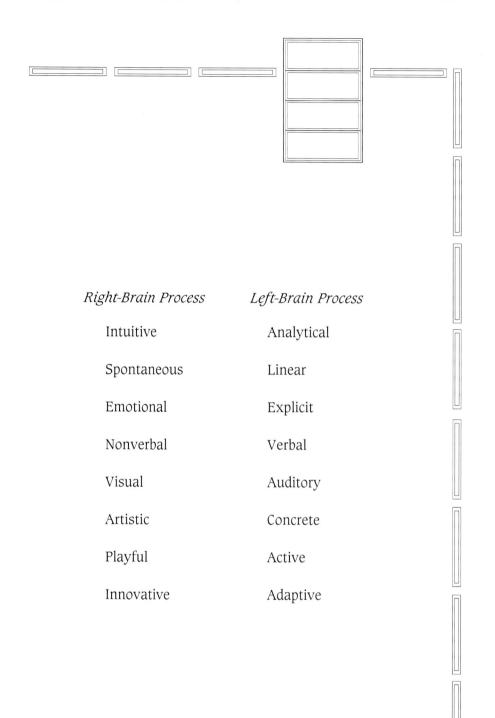

Right-Brain Process	*Left-Brain Process*
Intuitive	Analytical
Spontaneous	Linear
Emotional	Explicit
Nonverbal	Verbal
Visual	Auditory
Artistic	Concrete
Playful	Active
Innovative	Adaptive

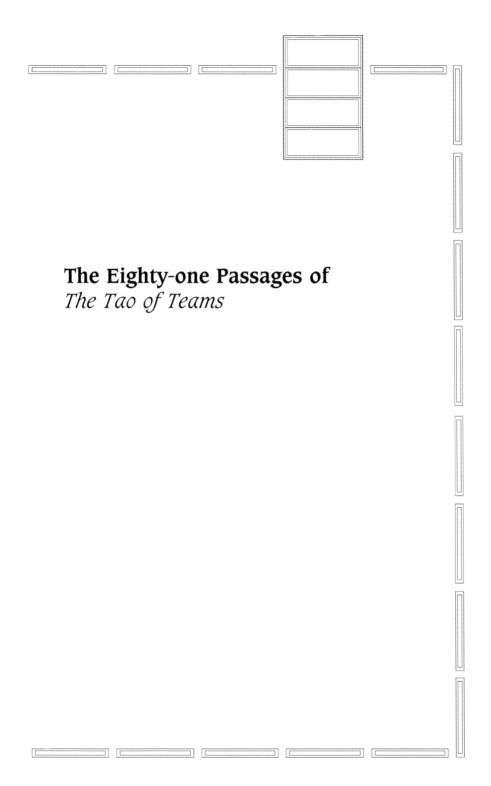

The Eighty-one Passages of
The Tao of Teams

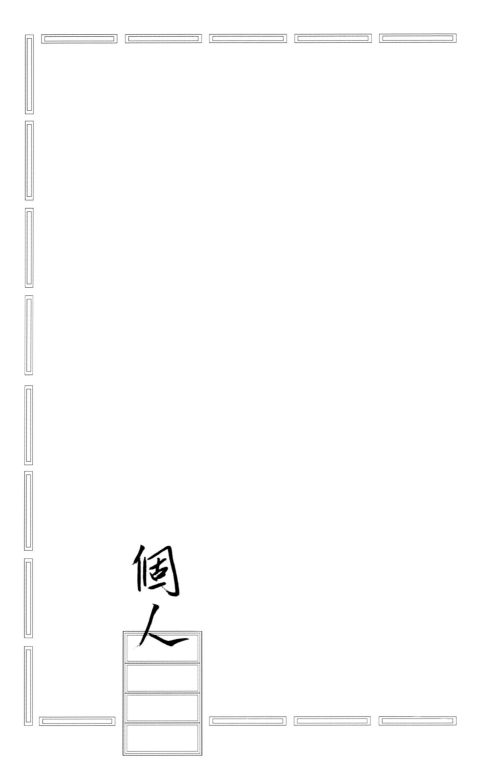

個人

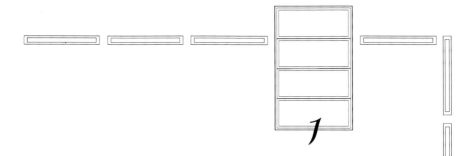

Individual Empowerment

The universe was created by the Absolute,
yet the Tao that can be spoken is not the
Tao that describes the Absolute.

The Tao evolved to support the beginning,
yet in its actions we see the ending.

The Absolute gave birth to all that we know.

It is matron of all that we know.

When the force of the Tao is focused,
complete power evolves.

The evolution of the Tao leads team members
to the beginning of individual awareness.

This is the journey to individual empowerment.

両極

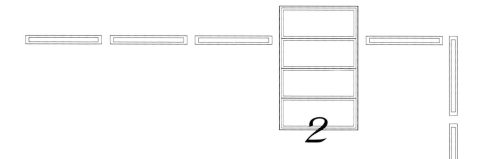

Polarity

While we may see our world as beautiful,
there are some who may see it as ugly.

While we may have had a bad experience,
there are those who are rejoicing in the good.

As in the world

> *Light and dark contrast each other.*
> *Love and hate define each other.*
> *Past and present follow each other.*

Therefore evolved team members

> Maintain their position without force.
> Speak without confusion.
> See all and miss nothing.
> Respond rather than react.
> Follow and lead.

This is the significance of polarity and its importance to the team.

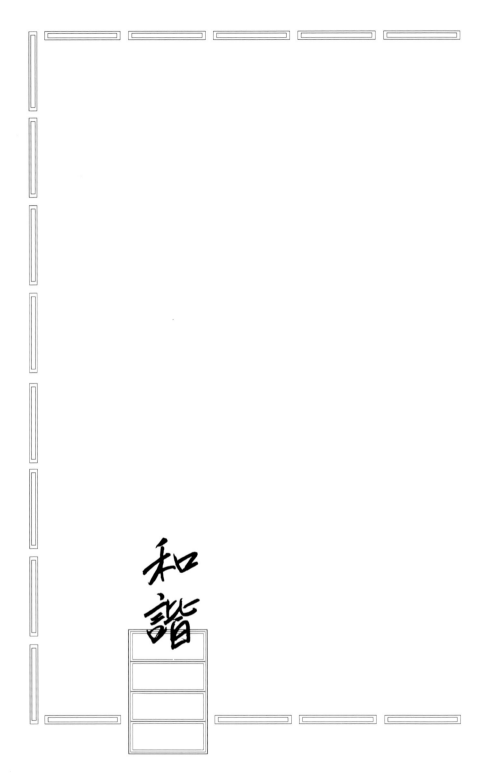

和諧

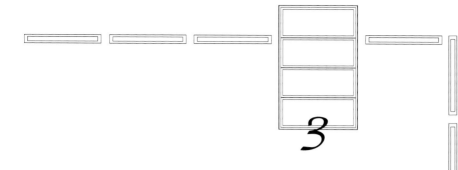

3

Harmony and Growth

Do not praise one over another, and
team members will not strive in opposition.
Do not indulge in wishful thinking, and
team members' minds will remain focused.

Evolved team members know
> That attitudes speak louder than words.
> That self-respect is a motivating force.
> That valuing integrity builds support.
> That flexibility creates deep trust.
> That spontaneity creates team energy.

Let team members act without direction.
Let them act with direction.
Activity with direction and without direction
creates order from chaos.

This is the way to maintain harmony and
create growth on the team.

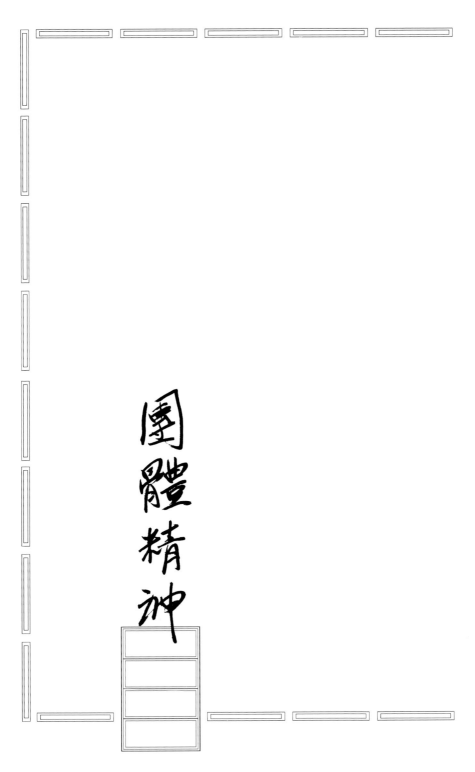

團體精神

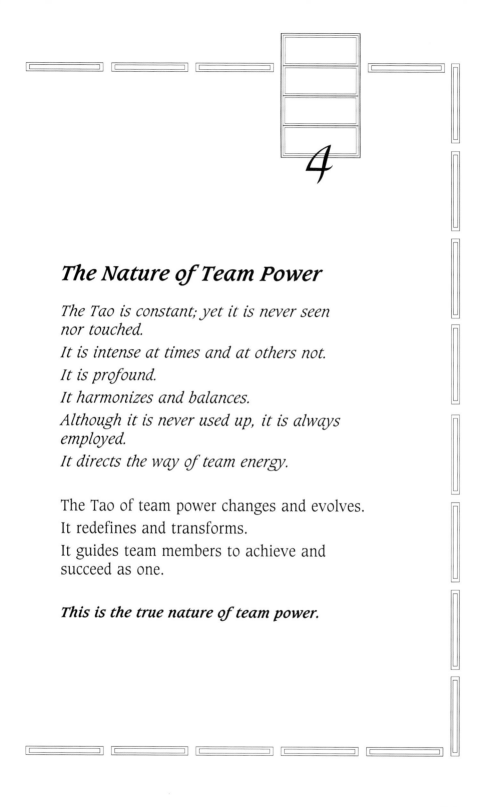

4

The Nature of Team Power

The Tao is constant; yet it is never seen nor touched.

It is intense at times and at others not.

It is profound.

It harmonizes and balances.

Although it is never used up, it is always employed.

It directs the way of team energy.

The Tao of team power changes and evolves.

It redefines and transforms.

It guides team members to achieve and succeed as one.

This is the true nature of team power.

良知

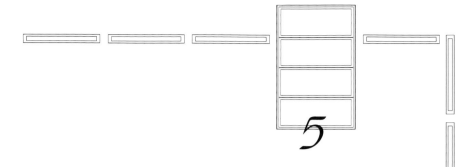

Conscience and Equity

The Tao is fair; it regards one as the other.

Forces change and bodies differ, but not the power of the Tao.

Success requires compassion not intolerance; independence not dependence; love not hate.

Evolved team members act impartially.

They see themselves in others.

Too much undirected activity and discussion will ultimately exhaust itself.

It is better for team members to remain focused.

Successful team members respect one another's individual conscience and strive to maintain equity in the team.

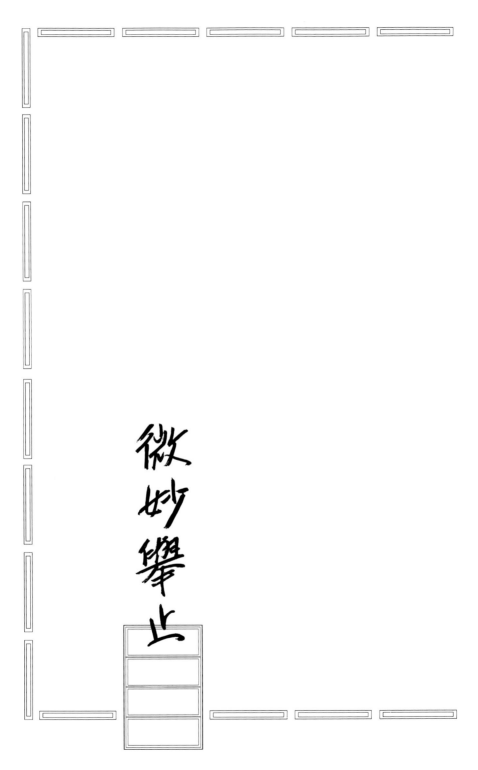

微妙擧止

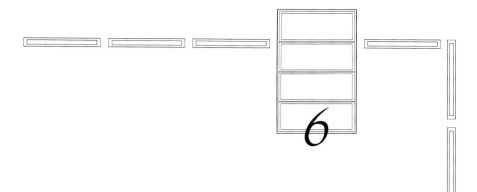

Subtle Behavior

The Tao is tranquil, while ever powerful.
It is neither overt nor covert; yet in its subtle
way it responds effortlessly.

Evolved team members who learn to dance
with the Tao recognize that their labors
can be completed effortlessly.

**This is how subtle behavior achieves
team goals.**

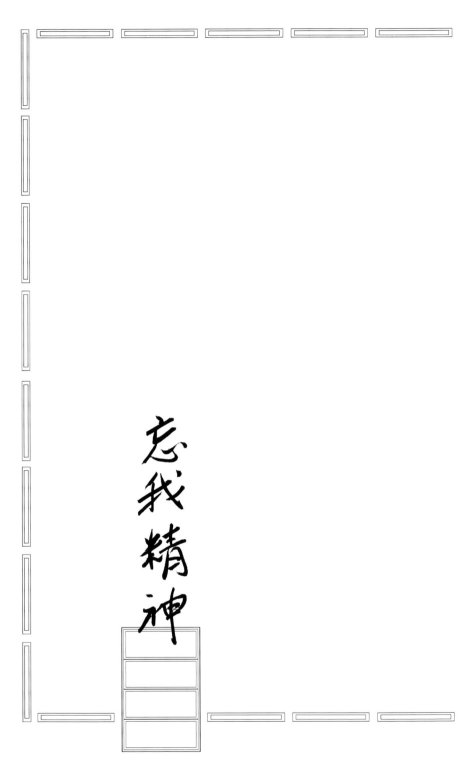

忘我精神

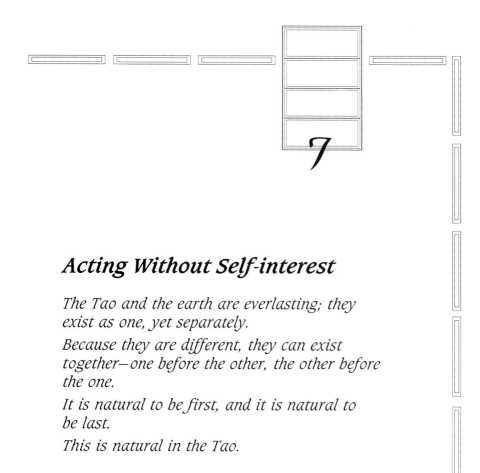

Acting Without Self-interest

The Tao and the earth are everlasting; they exist as one, yet separately.

Because they are different, they can exist together—one before the other, the other before the one.

It is natural to be first, and it is natural to be last.

This is natural in the Tao.

When evolved team members put themselves last, they will be first.

When they put themselves outside, they will be the first to be brought back inside.

Position in the flow occurs without force, and it endures.

This is how acting without self-interest helps the team succeed.

清晰

28

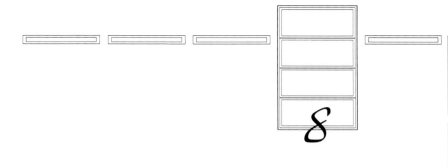

Clarity of Values

*The image of moving water suggests an
effortless flow that is yielding while
supporting all things.*
*Unlike water, values can clash, creating
resentment and mistrust—the ebb and the flow.*

When team members yield, others do not resist.

When team members insist, others do not yield.

Evolved team members do not confront opposing
values; they recognize them as personal beliefs.

To compete is to challenge, and efforts to win
yield only loss.

Learning is in discussion.

Strength is in collaboration.

In reality, that is the Tao; the answer lies in
knowing what is important to you.

**Thus clarity of values contributes to
team solidarity.**

進歩

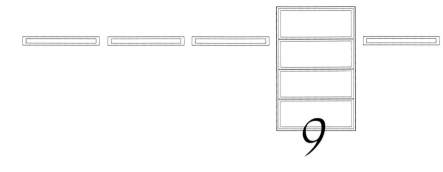

Move Forward After Success

*Dwelling in team success dismisses
eventual demise.*

*Resting with good fortune ignores decline;
however, pride in a task accomplished
cannot protect for long.*

Evolved team members

> Recognize that nothing is static in the Tao.

> Know that to stop and admire one's
> accomplishments for too long fosters decline.

> Recognize that when the job is finished,
> they must move on to the next task.

The Tao, like accomplishment, is energy
constantly flowing, never static, never ending.

**This knowledge helps all team members move
forward when the team has achieved success.**

平衡

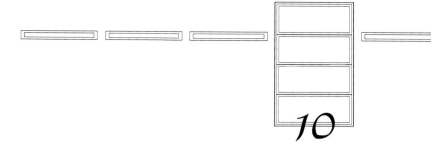

The Quest for Harmony and Inner Balance

*Within the Tao, we strive to maintain balance
but tend toward a state of imbalance.*

We attempt to see clearly, but our vision is blurred.

*We attempt to clear our thoughts but
experience confusion.*

*This is the challenge of the Tao—the constant
reconciliation of extremes.*

Resolving inner conflicts can be achieved

> *When balance is restored.*

> *When polarities unite as one.*

> *When one becomes the other.*

This is inner peace and the way of the Tao.

Evolved team members

> Succeed at what they attempt.

> See reality through an objective eye.

> Move beyond their own needs and become
> masters of their own future.

**This is the quest for harmony and a team
member's search for inner balance.**

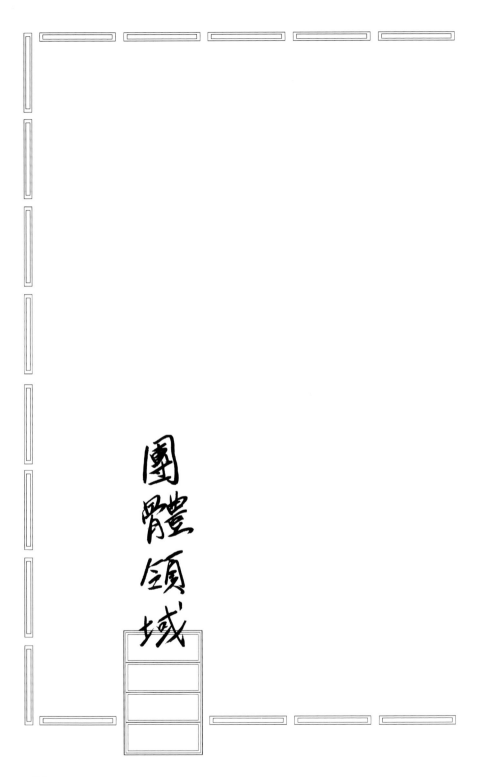

團體領域

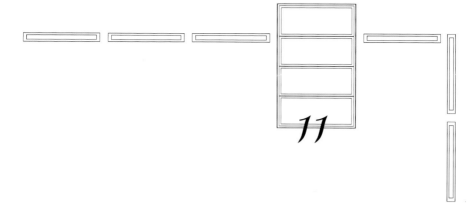

Using the Team's Field

Energy appears but cannot be seen.
It is sensed but cannot be touched.
It creates movement but cannot be manipulated.
It is present but elusive.
The silence creates the team field.
It is spirit and energy moving back and forth.
It is time and space that cannot be tracked.
For success, absence must be created, and it is
the absence that must be resolved.

When the team's force is focused, critical mass develops. When force is diffused energy is lost.

Evolved team members know to use the force that is there, by making use of what is not.

This is power when using the team's field.

品格

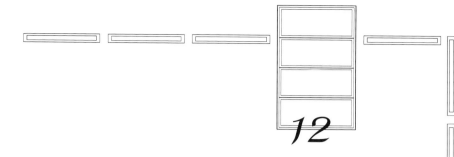

Team-Member Character

Many colors blind perceptions.
Many sounds interfere with hearing.
Many emotions jade feelings.
Too much sensory input blocks inner perception.
Shut out the input from without.
Focus on the calm within.
True freedom comes from controlling
the senses.

Evolved team members

> Cultivate their intuitive mind.
>
> Limit their worldly desires.
>
> Free themselves from the need for praise.
>
> Detach themselves from the fear of blame.

When these truths are acknowledged, internal
understanding begins.

Managed sensory input assures
team-member character.

自制

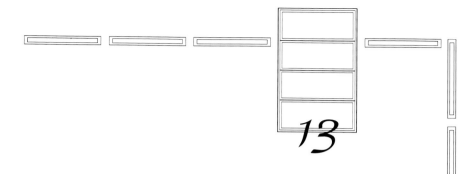

Mastering Self

Achievement and failure offer warnings.
Winning and losing are identified with the self.
When we reach new heights, we feel exposed.
When we do not succeed, we feel that we are
failures.
The reason for our alarm is not knowing self.
The reason for our rejoicing is knowing self.
When we know self, what is there to fear?

Evolved team members
  Know themselves.
  Trust their intuitive instincts.
  Commit to working within the Tao.

Mastering self is a team member's beginning.

識道

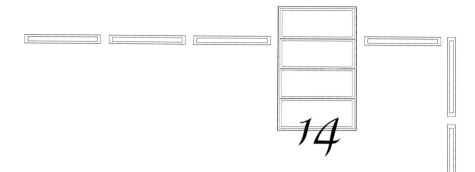

Knowing the Tao

Nameless, the Tao is called by many names.
Formless, its name assumes many shapes.
The Tao is strived for but never attained.
It cannot be named.
It cannot be seen.
It cannot be achieved.

The Tao lives in the minds of all team members.
The Tao can only be seen in the way they live
their lives and how they impact the world
around them.
Evolved team members
> Understand the simple patterns of life.
> Can facilitate their future.
> Can control their reality.

**Thus knowing the Tao is a team
member's primer.**

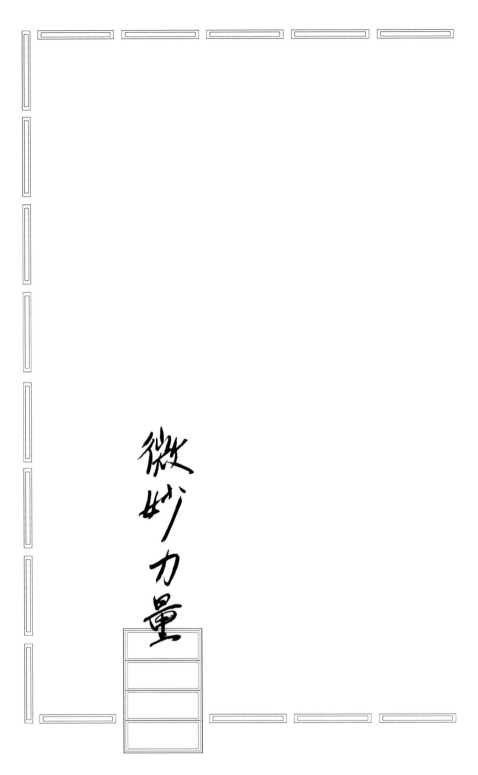

微妙力量

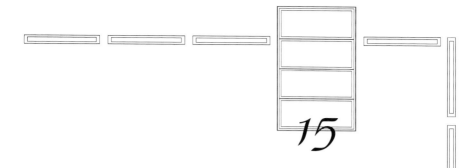

Subtle Power

*Team members who understand the Tao
are unique and thoroughly intuitive.*

Their energy is so pure, it cannot be understood.

*Since their energy cannot be understood, it
cannot be restrained.*

Evolved team members know that

> The more subtle the use of power, the
> greater its effect.

> The greater their stability, the less
> resistance they will encounter.

> The more integrated they are in their
> environment, the less the need to show
> obvious power.

***In order to facilitate harmony on the team,
team members must understand the potency
of subtle power.***

自然

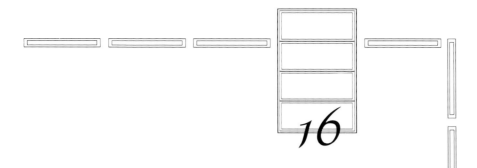

Acting Natural

Strive to be natural, and freedom will occur.

Be open and a part of all things, and the source of all things will set you free.

To comprehend the source is called knowledge; to have knowledge of the source is called insight; to have insight on the source is called destiny.

A team member's destiny lies in striving to be whole, in striving to be free, in striving to be one with the team.

Evolved team members act natural; they know the Tao.

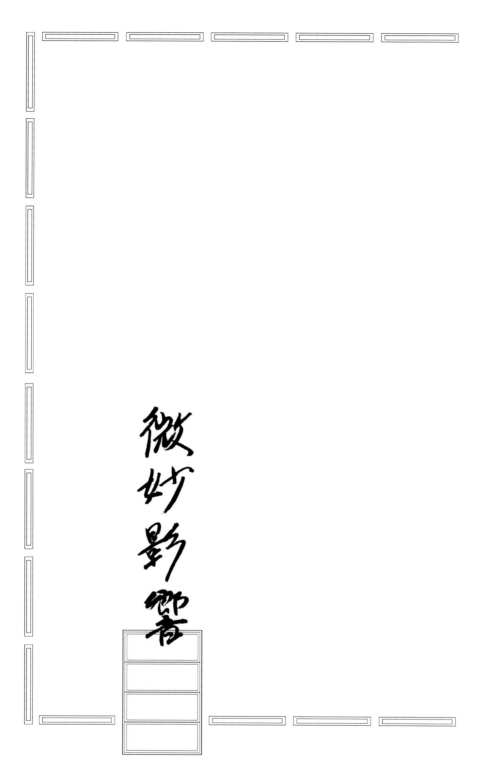

微妙影響

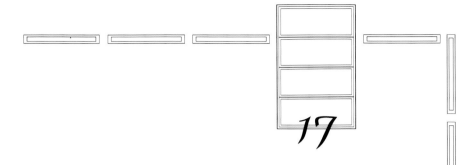

Leadership Is Subtle

Team leaders are effective when their influence is barely felt.
They are least effective when they are intrusive.

When team leaders are overbearing, the task becomes a burden.

When team leaders restrain themselves, the task of leading is done with ease.

With a leader's ease comes a deeper trust in the team.

And when there is trust, team members are content and more productive.

Rather than feeling led, they feel that they are following their own best instincts.

Team leadership is a subtle influence.

智慧

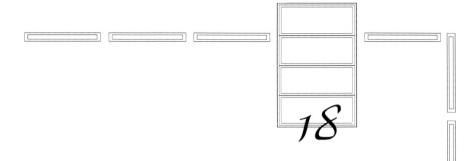

Following the Wisdom of the Tao

*When team members forget the Tao, strict
loyalty to the team is expected.*

*When the team forgets the Tao, adherence to
righteous behavior is fostered.*

*Teams that lose touch with their purpose
produce great hypocrisies.*

Evolved team members

> Know that adherence to the Tao is necessary.
>
> Understand that the Tao must always be
> considered.
>
> Recognize that the Tao always supports
> team efforts.

Teams must follow the wisdom of the Tao.

簡
單

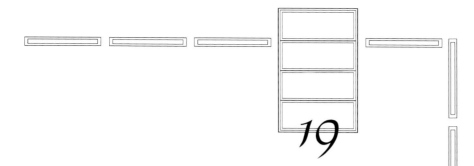

Simple Actions Reflect Commitment

Happiness comes in moments of purest simplicity.

Let go of the expectations that are placed upon
you; the team will benefit a hundredfold.

Discard the rules that others bestow on you;
tensions will ease and eventually disappear.

**Simple actions reflect a team member's
commitment.**

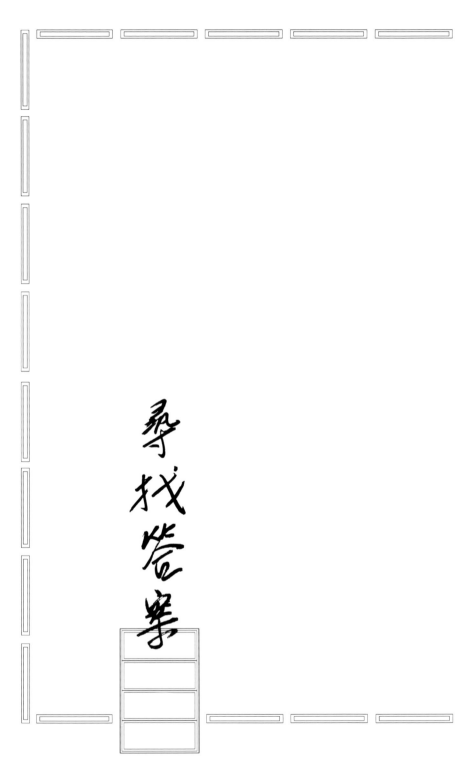

尋找答案

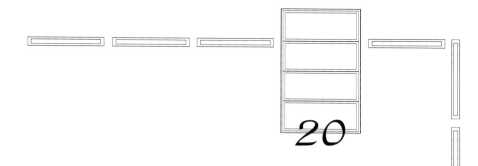

Seeking the Answer

Remain uncommitted to any doctrine, and answers will come.

Disregard the theoretical; intuition will make you aware.

Let go of dogma; the truth will guide you.

Evolved team members know that

Truth does not come from words alone.

Knowledge comes from direct experience.

Reality can only be translated intuitively.

Looking for what is certain requires that team members step outside their reality.

Seeking the answer is a team member's responsibility.

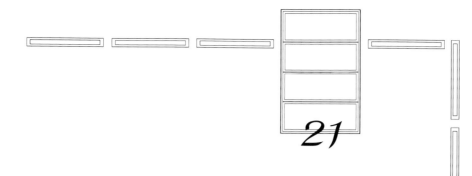

The Origin of Team Power

Team power cannot be experienced through the senses; it can only be known by its effect on others.

Team power is an informed force that impacts team members who are knowledgeable.

The origin of team power can only be known through an intuitive experience, similar to the laws that govern the universe.

Thus evolved team members consider the interdependent connections of all team relationships.

The origin of team power can only be experienced intuitively.

群力

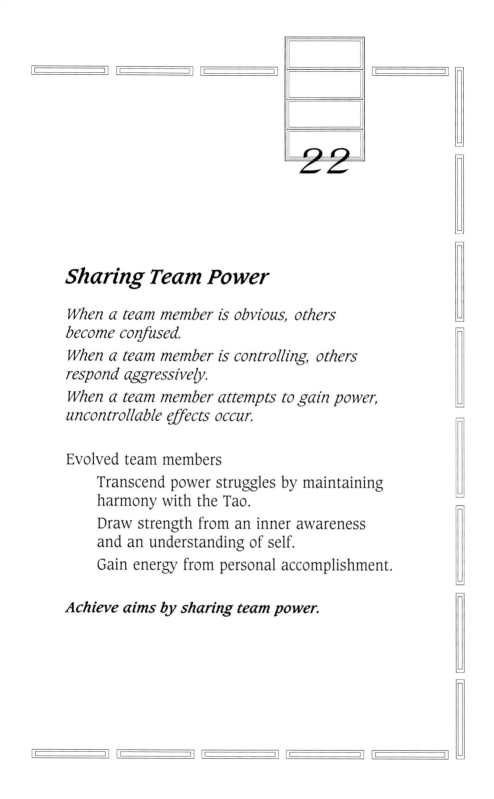

Sharing Team Power

When a team member is obvious, others become confused.

When a team member is controlling, others respond aggressively.

When a team member attempts to gain power, uncontrollable effects occur.

Evolved team members

> Transcend power struggles by maintaining harmony with the Tao.

> Draw strength from an inner awareness and an understanding of self.

> Gain energy from personal accomplishment.

Achieve aims by sharing team power.

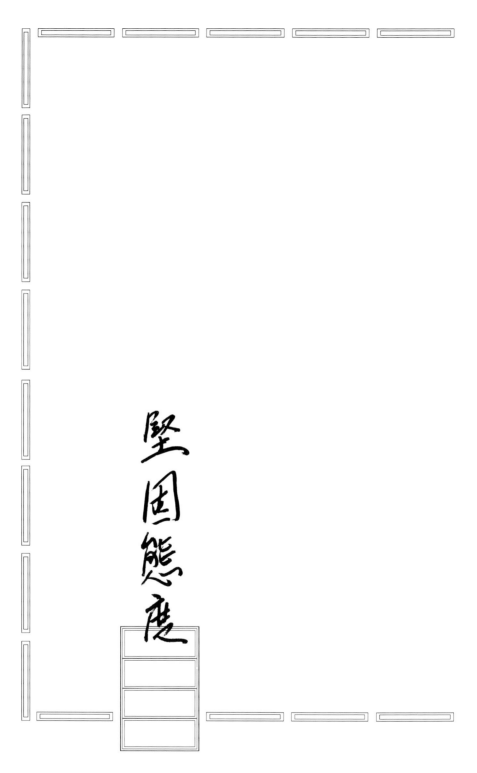

堅固態應

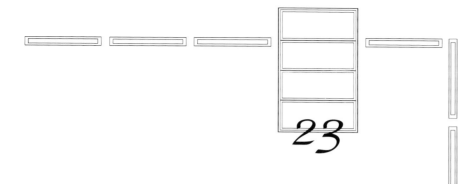

Attitude Is a Steady Force

*In nature, the thunder shower lasts a short
time, the trembling of the earth only a
few moments.*

*If the earth cannot sustain these forces without
responding, how can team members sustain
force without reacting?*

*In the Tao, belligerent movement toward
one's goals has little effect.*

Confrontation yields resistance.

Harmony yields a positive attitude.

The team member

> Who is steady, understands the Tao.

> Who admits to failure, knows success.

> Who comprehends self, recognizes reality.

> Who knows that what one believes one
> becomes, contributes powerfully to the team.

Attitude is a steady team-member force.

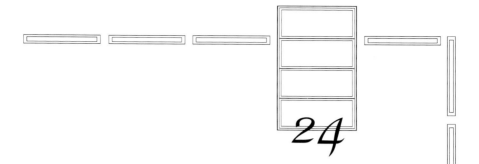

Excessive Behavior

Those who stay with the natural force of the Tao reject excess.

Those who possess the Tao know the richness of inner-focused behavior.

Team members who boast of success will be thought of as self-indulgent.

Team members who attempt to gain notoriety will be viewed as self-serving.

Team members who behave excessively will be considered unstable.

Excessive team-member behavior can be dangerous.

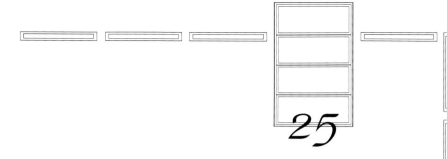

The Four Great Powers

*Before reality, a force existed that bound
all things together—silent, independent,
and never changing.*

It was regarded as the matron of the world.

Its name was unknown but was called the Tao.

Requiring a description, it was called omniscient.

*It runs through all things, and it returns to the
beginning of all things.*

Evolved team members intuitively recognize
the force of the Tao and how it flows through
the team.

Those who know and follow the Tao find
harmony and fulfillment.

**The four great powers that teams are built
on include the team members themselves,
leadership that is shared, the earth that
sustains us, and the Tao.**

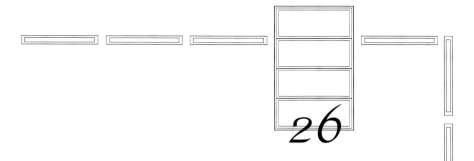

Remaining Centered

Centered team members know who they are and what they stand for; they can work with anyone and be successful.

They move forward; they move back.

They question, and they answer.

They support, and they are supported.

Thus evolved team members create a calm that serves as the foundation of the team.

The importance of remaining centered as a team member is to provide a foundation for the team.

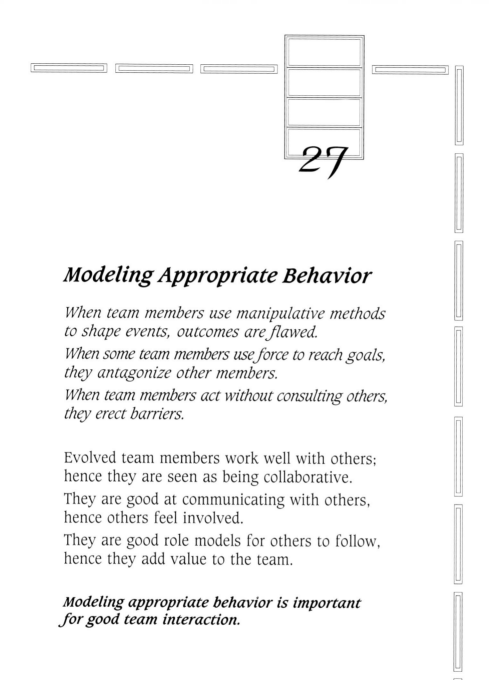

Modeling Appropriate Behavior

*When team members use manipulative methods
to shape events, outcomes are flawed.*

*When some team members use force to reach goals,
they antagonize other members.*

*When team members act without consulting others,
they erect barriers.*

Evolved team members work well with others;
hence they are seen as being collaborative.

They are good at communicating with others,
hence others feel involved.

They are good role models for others to follow,
hence they add value to the team.

**Modeling appropriate behavior is important
for good team interaction.**

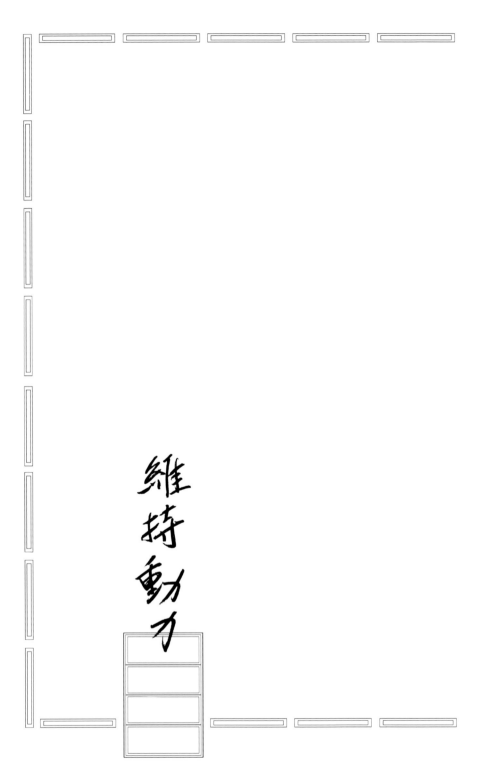

維持動力

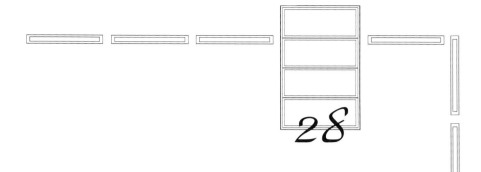

Managing Forces

Know the opposing forces in the universe;
become part of the flow.

By becoming part of the flow, power is not lost.

This is returning to the beginning.

Know the masculine and hold to the feminine.

Become part of the universal pattern.

By becoming part of the universal pattern,
power never wavers.

This is returning to the fullness of the Tao.

Evolved team members

> Direct others who otherwise would be
> without direction.

> Are subtle and modest in their use of power.

> Use simplicity to describe the energy that
> flows through the team.

Understanding leads to managing the forces
that govern team dynamics.

不干涉

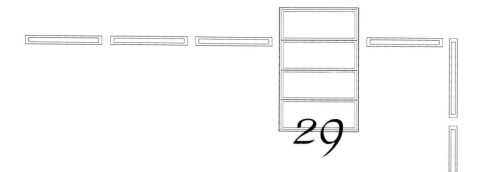

Noninterference

The team is dynamic; it is not to be manipulated.
Those who try, meet with failure.
Those who seize it, lose their grip.
To interfere with the team's natural state is
futile and often tragic.

Evolved team members
> Never push to extremes.
> Maintain emotional independence.
> Strive for intellectual balance.

Noninterference is one way to achieve team goals.

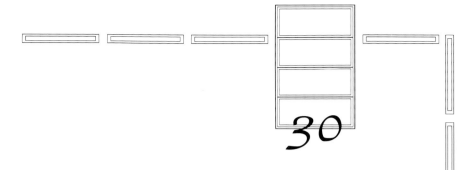

The Way to Lead

*Team leaders who understand group dynamics
exert minimal force to guide the team.*

Too much force produces an aggressive response.

Too little force creates chaos.

*Team leaders who use the Tao to guide team
members do not use forceful methods to manage
the team.*

Such methods create a backlash.

Evolved team leaders

    Succeed without boasting.

    Succeed without making claims.

    Succeed without arrogance.

This is the way team leaders lead.

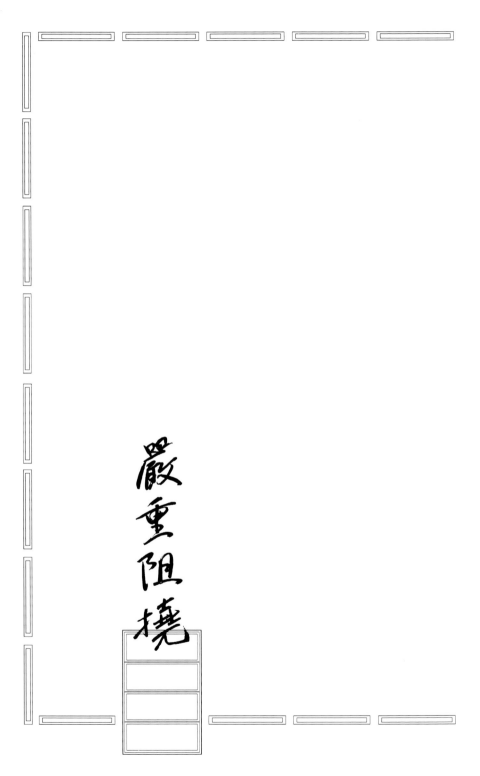

嚴重阻撓

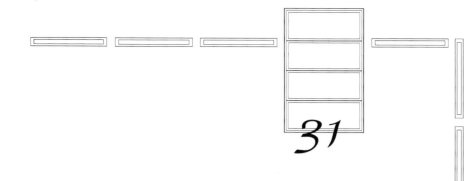

Interventions Create Discord

Severe interventions are actions of last resort.
When force is unavoidable, restraint is required.
When force is used, reactions are regrettable.
Conflicts are not to be applauded but to be facilitated.
They are not the ending, but rather the beginning.

Evolved team members
> Practice restraint.
> Experience the energy of engagement.
> Use energy to create change.

Severe interventions create team discord.

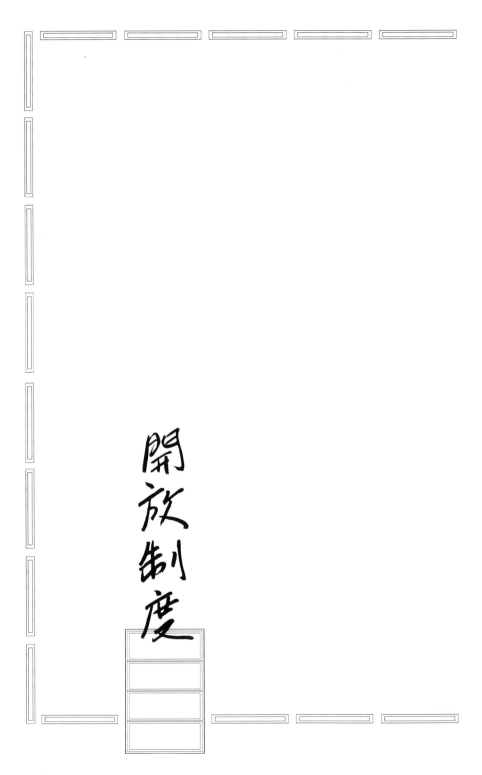

開放制度

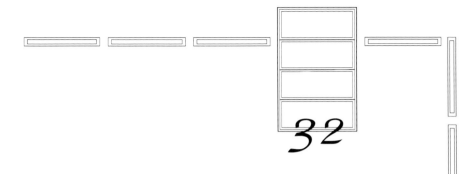

Maintaining an Open System

The Tao in its simplicity cannot be mastered,
nor can it be directed.

It cannot be perceived,
yet it contains innumerable universes.

If team members remain centered in the Tao, all
things stay in balance, and the team is open.

If team members act in the extreme,
disequilibrium occurs, and the team closes.

Evolved team members

> Move toward simplicity and away from
> complexity.

> Move toward relationships and away
> from differentiation.

> Create a supportive climate that allows
> team members to learn and grow.

This is the importance of maintaining the team
as an open system.

精通

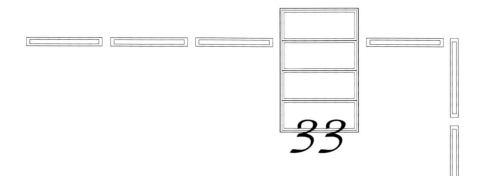

Mastery

Those who persevere achieve their ends.

Team members who influence others are
considered coaches.

Team members who know themselves are
considered intelligent.

Those who facilitate the work of others
have strength.

Those who manage themselves have character.

Mastery is a prime team-member accomplishment.

変化

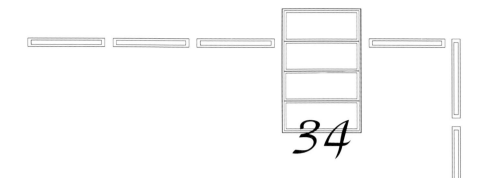

Diversity

Energy does not differentiate, it mediates all.

The energy is the Tao, the flowing force that maintains the universe.

The energy of the team is all around.

It is within, and it is without.

All team members depend on the energy for growth, and they are supported by it.

When all team members work together, a synergy occurs.

When differences are consolidated, team energy intensifies.

Unity in differences is how diversity works in the team.

意思

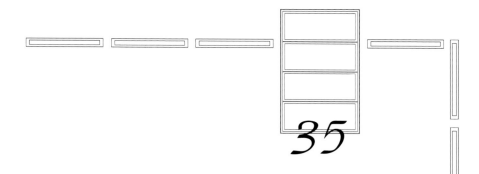

Creating Meaning

Maintain the image of the Tao, and all the world will follow, bringing only peace and stability.

This awareness leads to an awareness of the interconnection and interdependence of all things.

It is a state of mind, an experiment in thinking.

The evolved team member
> Experiences cohesion.
> Experiences integration.
> Experiences being one with the environment.

This is how team members create meaning.

政治

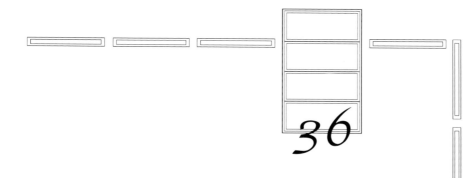

Team Politics

*In order for the team to be depleted, it must
be expanded.*

*In order for the team to be weakened, it must
be strengthened.*

*All actions reveal their opposite and seeing this
is called discerning insight.*

Evolved team members

Know that the weak can overcome
the strong.

Know that excessiveness forces things to
grow into their opposites.

Recognize that advantage yields the
potential for loss.

This is knowing team politics.

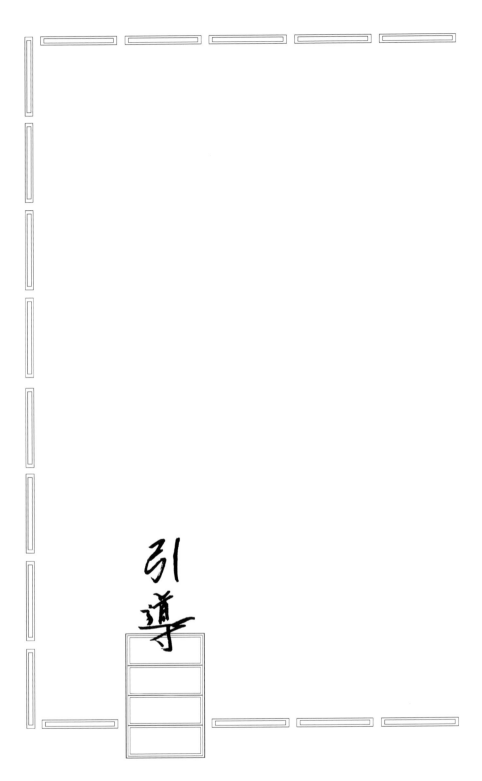

引導

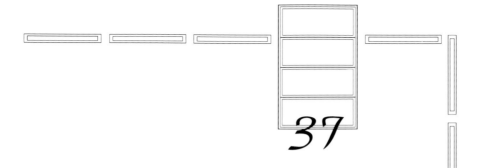

Guiding the Team

The Tao never bustles, yet it is always active.
It is subtle, yet it maintains its force.
If team leaders can hold onto the Tao, the team
will be naturally and positively influenced.

Evolved team leaders

> Maintain emotional balance.
>
> Exude intellectual strength.
>
> Put their energies into leading, not interfering
> with the lives of team members.
>
> Influence naturally, without opposition
> or animosity.

This is how team leaders effectively guide
the team.

謙讓

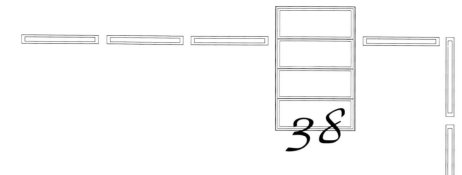

Leadership and Humility

*When team leaders obtain power, they become
like a great sea: all streams run into it.*

*The more power they obtain, the greater the
need for humility.*

*Humility means trusting the Tao, thus never
needing to be defensive.*

Good team leaders resemble good people;
when a mistake is made, it is realized.

Having realized it, team leaders admit it, and
having admitted it, they correct it.

Team leaders consider those who give them
feedback important resources.

They think of their opponents as the shadow
that they themselves cast.

**This is the significance of team leadership
and humility.**

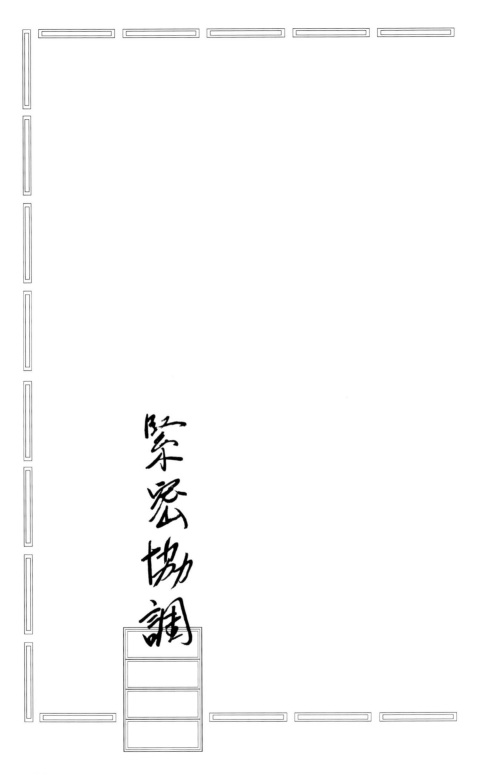

緊密協調

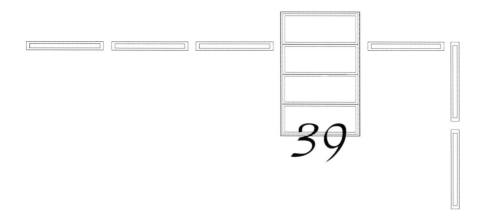

Leadership Is Harmony

Team leaders in harmony with the Tao know themselves.

They sense the rhythmic interactions of the team.

Team leaders in harmony with the Tao make team connections.

These are all attained through self-awareness.

When team leaders identify with team members, they reciprocate.

When team leaders gain power from the team, team members share responsibility.

When team leaders are incorruptible, team members offer support.

Effective team leadership is a cohesive harmony.

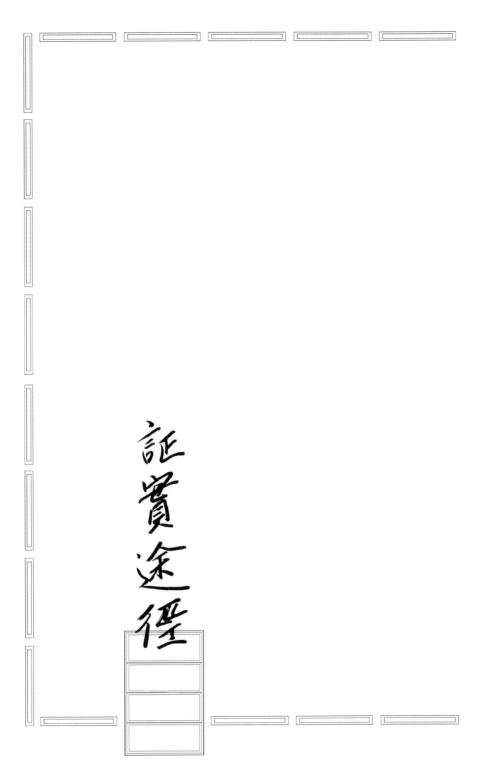

証賢途徑

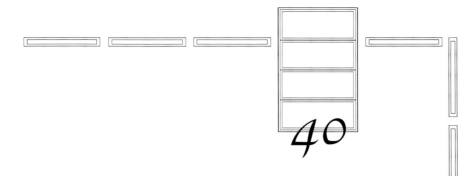

A Proven Path

The Tao originated in the Absolute, the matron of all things.

Positive and negative states originated from the Tao, the subtle force governing the universe.

These states created physical reality, a unified field of forces.

These forces reflect the way of the Tao.

Effective teams understand polarities, that they create cause and effect.

Effective teams understand cycles, that they make things easy or difficult.

Effective teams avoid extremes.

The team that is open and receptive gains power. This is a proven path for the team to follow.

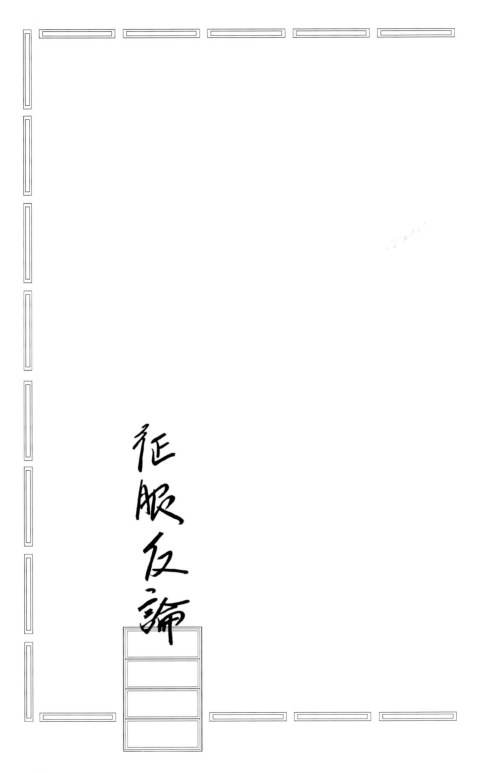

征服反論

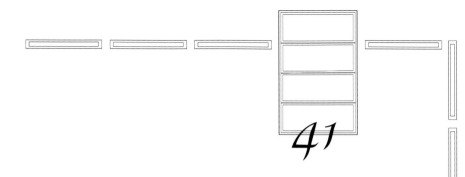

Mastering the Paradox

When respected team leaders learn of the Tao, they emulate it.

When mediocre team leaders hear of the Tao, they react to it.

When poor team leaders hear of the Tao, they laugh at it.

Yet without laughter, the Tao would not be known.

Evolved team leaders

> Seek out those who are intuitive and visionary.

> Recognize those who have evolutionary ideas.

> Support those who use innovative thinking.

> Have faith in those who recognize that reality is constantly changing.

> Admire those who adhere to the physical laws that govern the universe.

Team leaders must master the paradox.

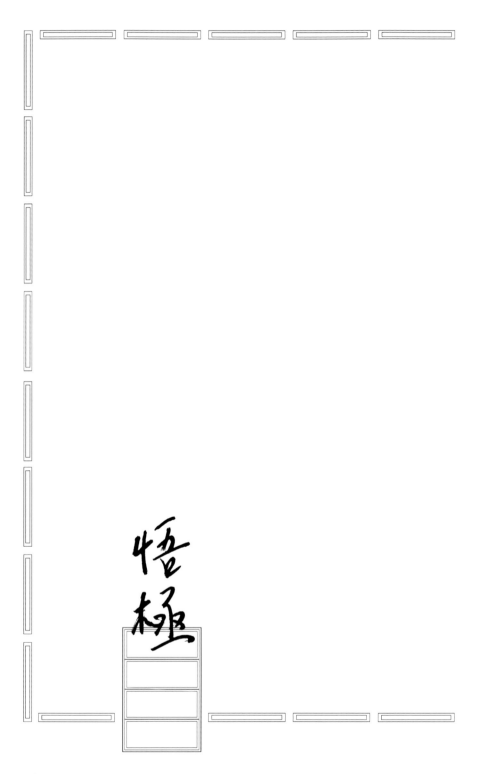

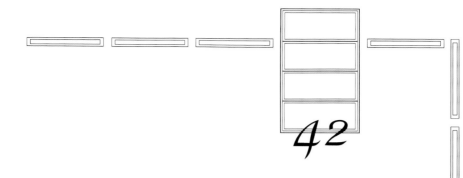

Understanding Polarity

The Absolute, standing outside of time and space, produced the Tao.

The Tao produced the One: temporal reality.

The One produced the Two: positive and negative charges.

The Two produced the Three: matter, energy, and the laws that hold them together.

These three things tell us all there is to know about the universe. Their blending brings harmony.

Evolved team leaders know that everything in the universe is interconnected and interdependent.

This is the origin of the behavior of polarity: when one thing decreases, something else increases.

Thus,

> To lead, team leaders must follow.
>
> To direct, team leaders must take direction.
>
> To endure, team leaders must not put themselves above others.

Team leaders must understand polarity.

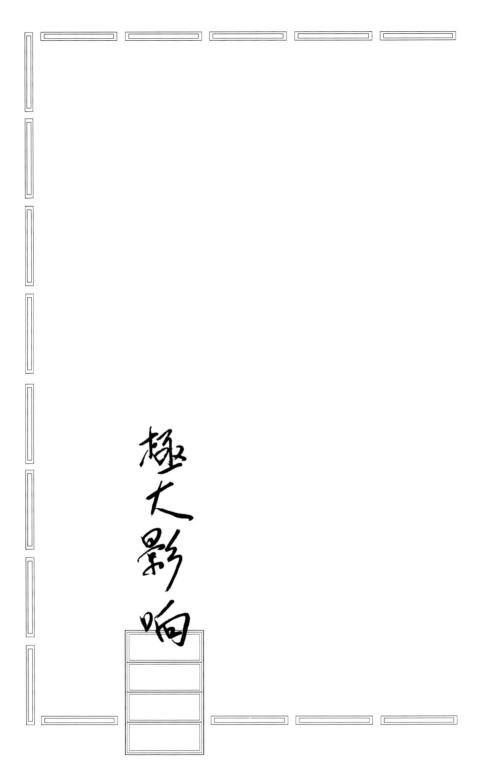

极大影响

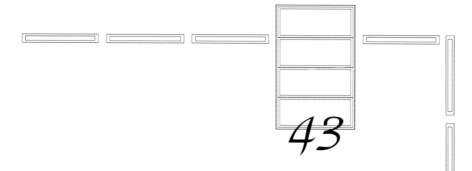

Subtle Use of Power

*Problems in teams arise from strong reactions
to larger influences.*

*Problems dissipate when they are not met with force
but rather invited to stay.*

Evolved team members know that

> In yielding, team members overtake.

> In the absence of action, team members
> maintain the advantage.

> In speaking softly, team members are heard.

**When action is necessary, the subtle use of
power gives the team greater influence.**

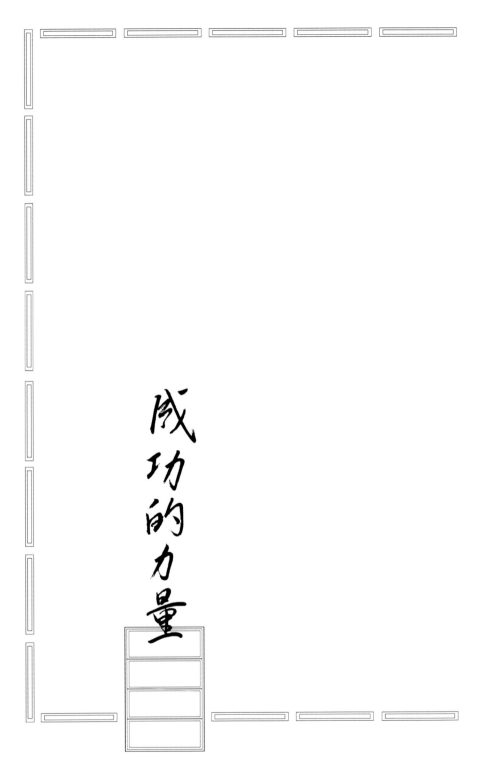

成功的力量

44

Being Successful by Needing Less

Team members who identify themselves with worldly goods create imbalance in the world.

Team members who attach themselves to material things do not evolve intellectually.

They view temporal space as fixed and unchanging.

This view is adaptive and closed, not generative and open.

Evolved team members know that

> There is greater power in being unburdened by material things.

> There is greater power in letting things pass.

The greatest power lies with team members who are movable, unburdened, and independent.

Team members can be successful needing less.

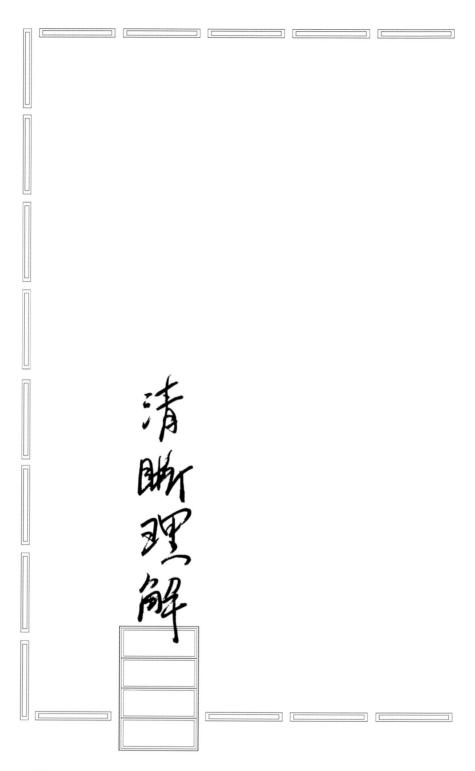

清晰理解

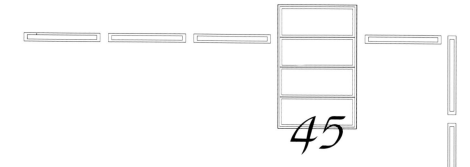

Clarity of Perception

When a cup is empty, it is most useful.

When accomplishment is open-ended, it generates growth.

When achievement is incomplete, its usefulness is greatest.

When team members achieve balance, they contribute to team development.

Evolved team members know that clarity of perception brings order to the team.

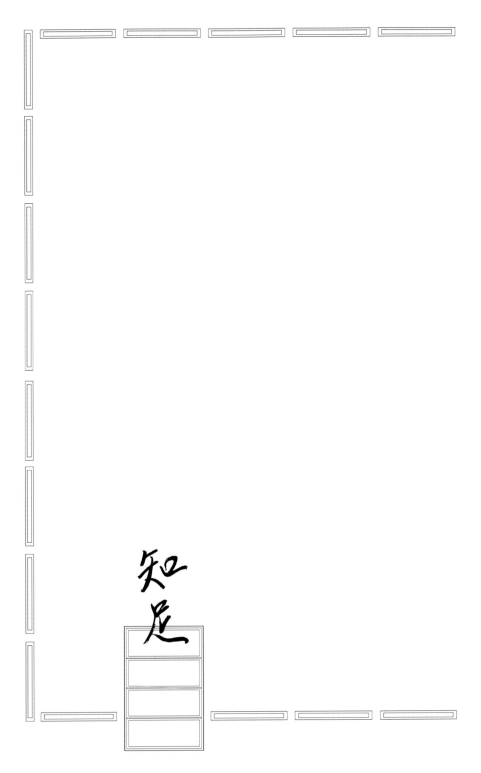

知足

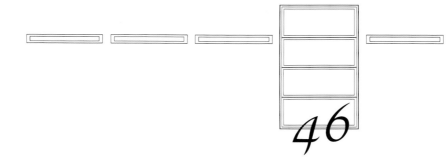

Knowing When Enough Is Enough

*Team members who do not understand the Tao
look outward for the meaning of life.*

*Team members following the Tao look inward
for the meaning of existence.*

*They know when enough is enough and avoid
being greedy.*

When the force of the Tao is possessed, the
team develops superior qualities.

When the force of the Tao is not present, the
team develops no purpose nor meaning.

**Evolved team members must know when
enough is enough.**

速進成功

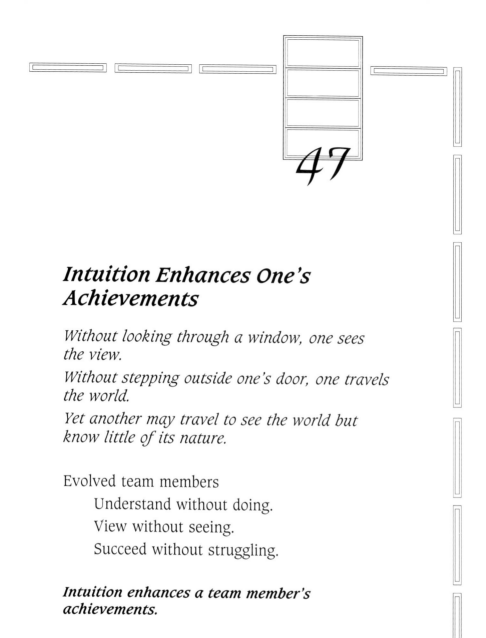

Intuition Enhances One's Achievements

Without looking through a window, one sees the view.

Without stepping outside one's door, one travels the world.

Yet another may travel to see the world but know little of its nature.

Evolved team members
> Understand without doing.
> View without seeing.
> Succeed without struggling.

Intuition enhances a team member's achievements.

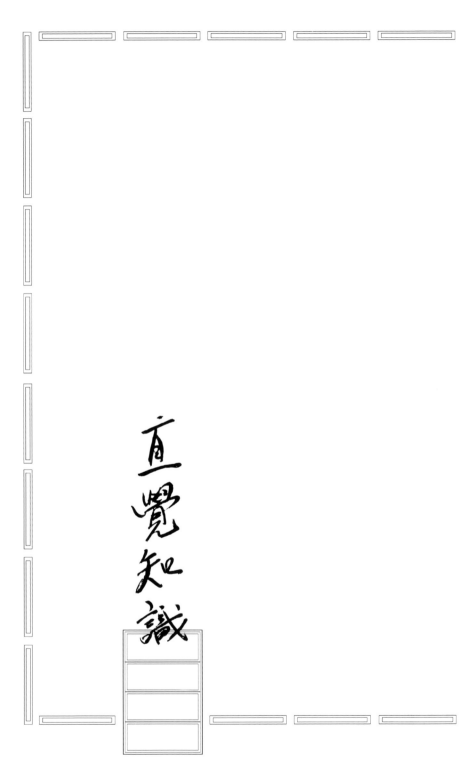

直覺知識

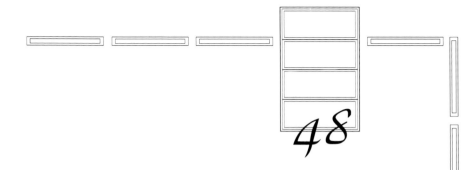

Pure Information Refines Instinctive Knowledge

The constant pursuit of ideas yields powerful insights, but the fixation on some ideas limits one's thinking.

When one uses effort to elicit information, a contaminated form of reality emerges.

When one does not interfere, pure information is collected.

Evolved team members understand that

Pure information refines a team member's instinctive knowledge.

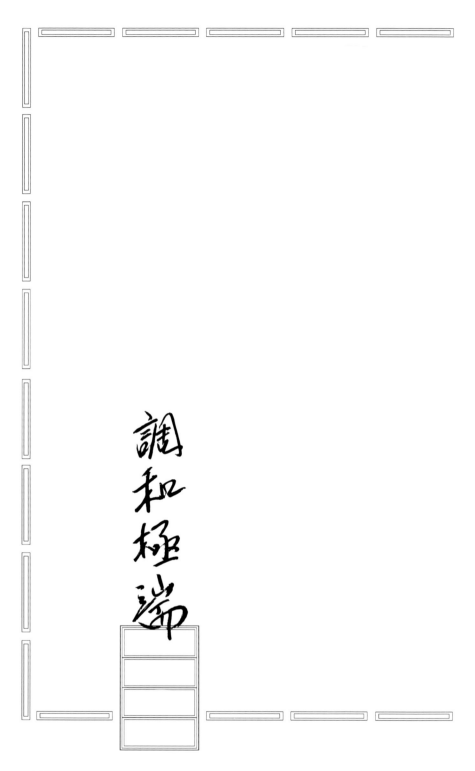

調和極端

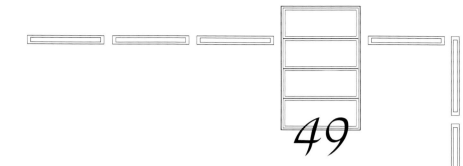

Neutralizing Extremes Creates Balance

Team members with fixed ideas distort information.

Team members with impartial thoughts enhance ideas.

Relying on information gained from sight and sound alone is limiting, but looking to the future with an open heart is expanding.

Evolved team members

> Trust those who cannot be trusted.
>
> Like those who are not likable.
>
> Seek out those who are not accessible.

Neutralizing extremes balances the team.

循環

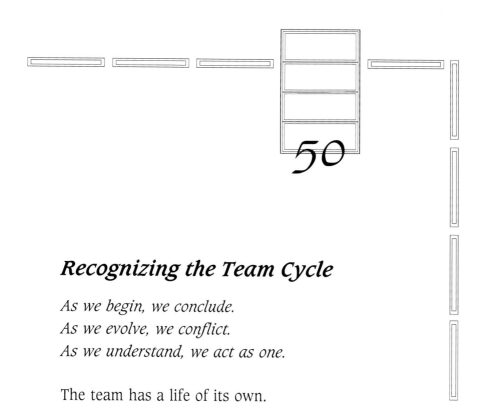

Recognizing the Team Cycle

As we begin, we conclude.
As we evolve, we conflict.
As we understand, we act as one.

The team has a life of its own.

Recognizing the team cycle contributes to team-member knowledge.

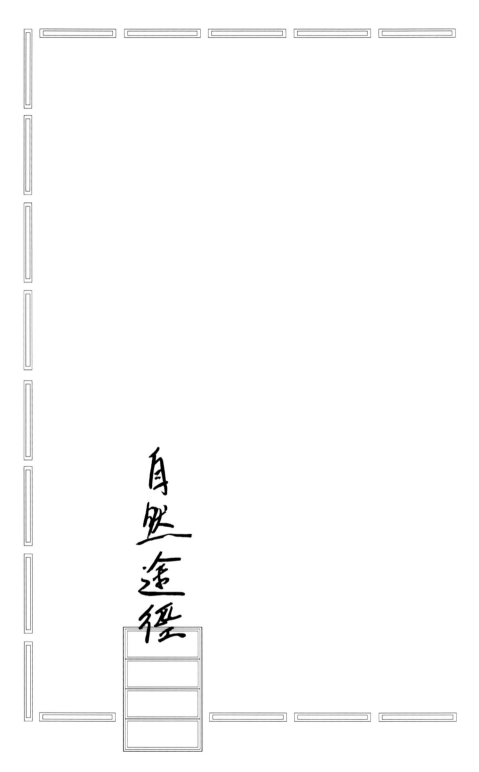

自然途徑

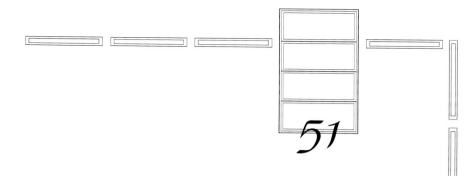

A Natural and Spontaneous Path

The Tao's existence yields.
The Tao's influence supports.
The Tao's principles fashion.
All three elements contribute completely.

Team members in harmony with the Tao find support for their deeds.

Those not in harmony with the Tao have difficulty achieving their goals.

Respecting the Tao and valuing its power is essential; yet, it is neither demanded nor expected. It must come naturally.

Evolved team members

> Maintain an unbiased attitude.
>
> Emulate the principles of the Tao.
>
> Shape their own destiny.

Teams who reveal the force of the Tao follow a natural and spontaneous path.

邏
輯

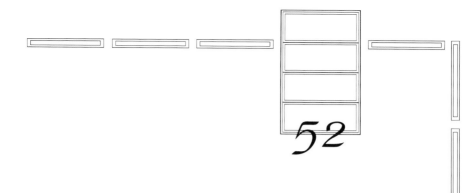

Using the Intuitive and the Logical Mind

Those who close off their senses prevent input.

Those who are open to sensory input lose themselves in worldly pursuits.

Each method by itself yields less than satisfactory results.

Evolved team members

> Enhance their external perception of the world with information generated from the intuitive mind.
>
> Develop a sense of the changing processes and patterns in life.
>
> Allow their minds to evolve.

Effective team members use both the intuitive and the logical mind.

平衡

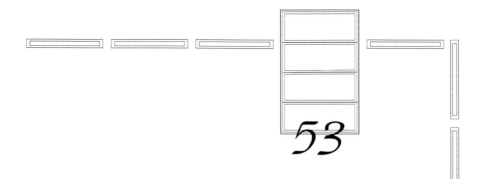

Unbalanced Teams Do Not Survive

Following the Tao means listening to the inner voice and ultimately perceiving social and environmental realities.

Following the Tao means holding to the path of least resistance, a path strewn with many tempting detours.

These temptations are excessive ambition and other desires that can divide the team.

If team members are diverted, they can block their own personal growth and endanger the survival of the team.

A divided team acts aggressively toward its members.

Unbalanced teams act against the nature of the Tao.

Unbalanced teams do not survive.

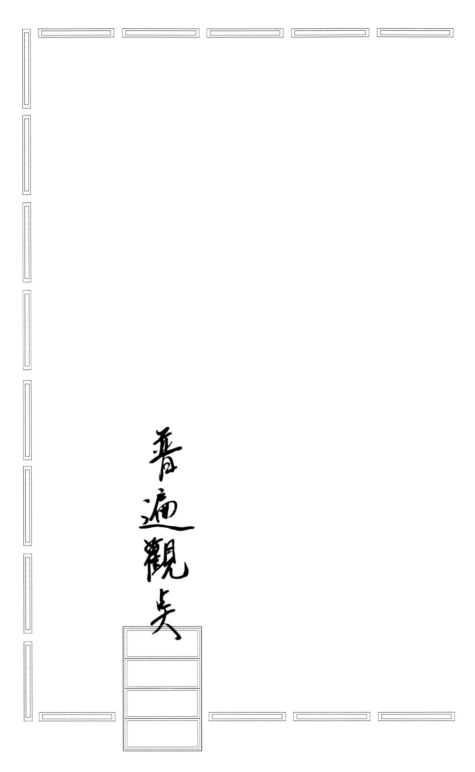

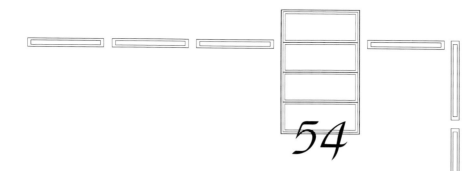

Developing a Universal Perspective

Cultivate self-awareness; its power is real.

Develop the team; its power increases.

Cultivate the organization; its power becomes abundant.

Develop the community; its power brings people together.

Cultivate the world; its power is beyond comprehension.

Thus team members must develop a universal perspective.

A universal understanding begins with self-awareness; it facilitates the interconnectedness of all things.

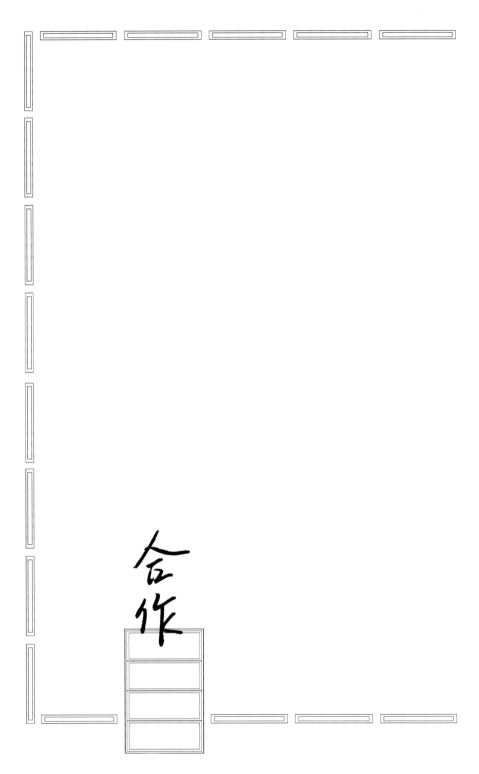

合作

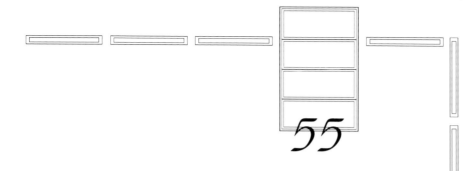

Team Power Is Found in Working Together

Team members who experience the Tao are like young children, acting spontaneously and seeking new learning situations.

They do not compete.

They do not attack.

They are protected.

Evolved team members are marked by spontaneity and use this response like a martial art form to protect themselves.

When team members are pushed, they yield; this response throws their attacker off balance.

When team members work together, they hold their position of power.

Unbalanced power is not stable and soon dissipates.

Team power is found in working together.

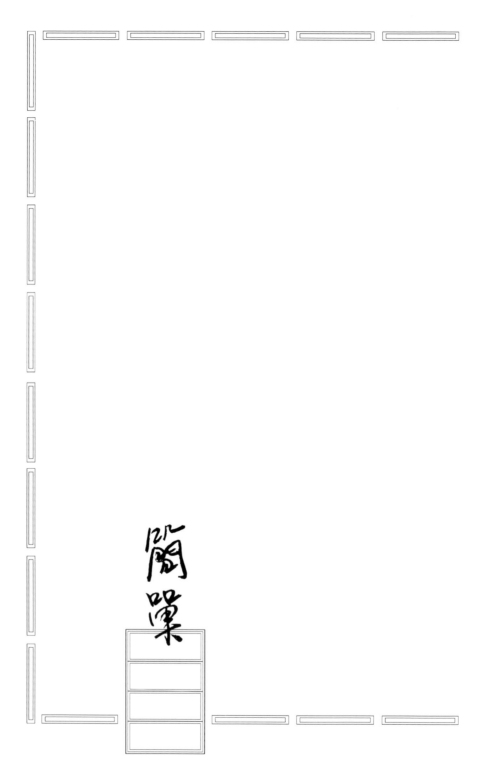

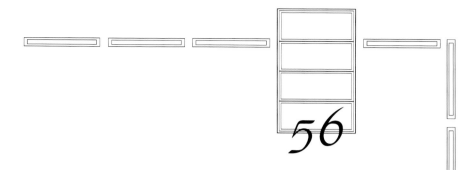

Simplicity Contributes to Personal Power

Knowledge based on teachings from outside the inner mind is limiting.

Knowledge based on inner awareness contributes to an understanding of the universe.

Cultivating intuition promotes intellectual independence.

Evolved team members

Neutralize belligerent behavior.

Clarify their strategies.

Harmonize with needs of the environment.

Achieve oneness with the universe.

Simplicity contributes to a team member's personal power.

阻止

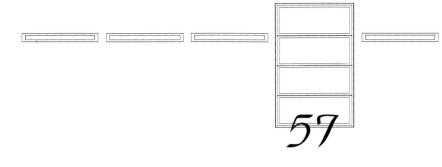

57

Leading Without Interference

Too many rules lead to inadequacy.

An exaggerated emphasis on morality leads to immoral behavior.

Too much control leads to cunning and sly reactions.

Team leaders should

    Lead with correctness.

    Facilitate with openness.

    Manage the process with effortlessness.

Evolved team leaders

    Do not meddle when it can be avoided.

    Remain calm in turbulent situations.

    Offer support in a collaborative fashion.

    Subdue ambitious desires.

In this way, the team is favorably influenced.

Team leaders lead without interference.

發揮

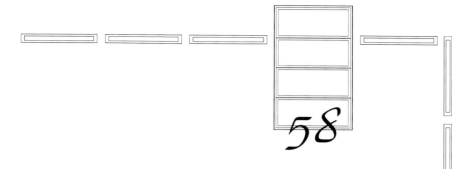

Micromanagement Causes
a Counteraction

*If the team is managed fairly, it will respond
with great productivity.*

*If the team is regulated severely, it will respond
with great discontent.*

*Since it is the nature of people to resist repression,
it must be avoided.*

Evolved team members

> Understand and avoid extremes.

> Intelligently shape the team without
> excessive control.

> Cultivate themselves and become role
> models for other team members.

**Micromanagement of the team will cause
a counteraction.**

温和

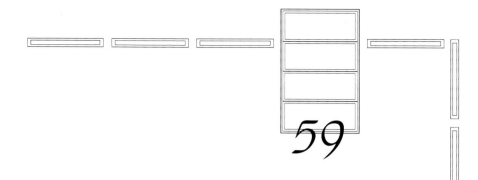

Moderation

When leading the team, there is nothing more important than moderation.

Since moderation means avoiding excess, it is the process that empowers.

When appropriate power is gained; all is possible.

When all is possible, there are no boundaries.

When there are no boundaries, the team can achieve new heights.

Evolved team leaders
    Have great influence.
    Develop effective teams.
    Endure and advance.

Moderation guides the team.

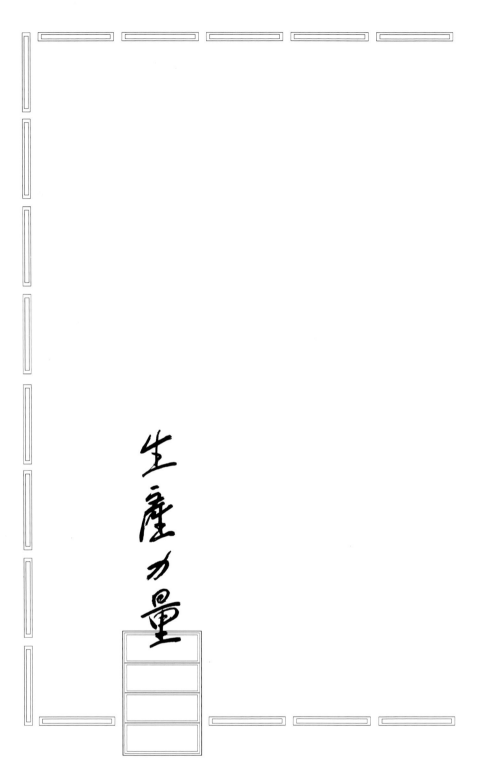

生產力量

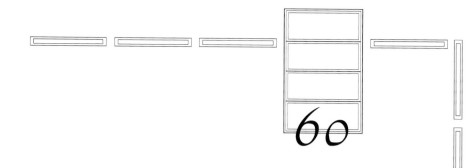

Productivity

*Leading a team is like cooking a small fish:
overcook the fish and it falls apart.*

Interference imperils one's position.

*When there are no effortless solutions, it is
appropriate to allow the Tao to point the way.*

*This is a natural way to achieve success and an
appropriate stance for empowering the team.*

The evolved team member must develop the Tao
in team affairs. Then many things will become
obvious.

**Productivity prevails when the team is not
manipulated.**

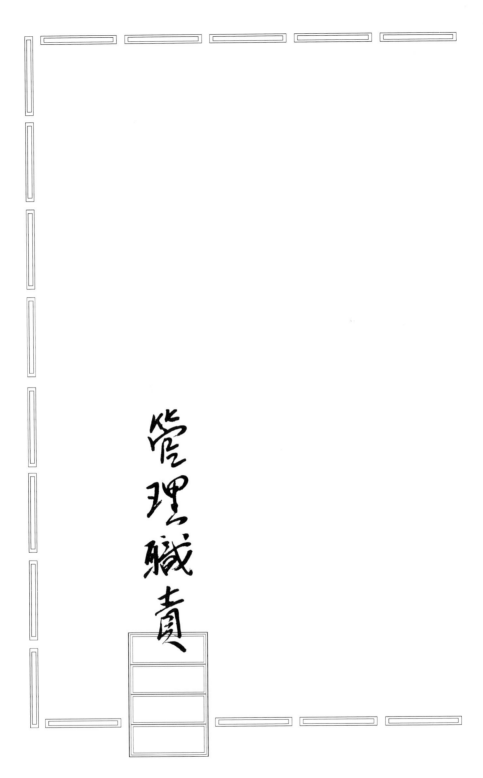

管理職責

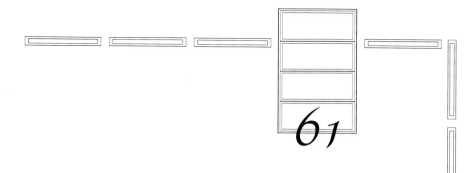

Stewardship

*The power that comes from serving others at
the individual, group, and organizational levels
makes all things possible.*

What the team desires is to unite and support
others, and what a team member desires is
to join and serve others.

This is a nonaggressive, noninterfering position
taken by team members who are naturally
diplomatic. This position is advantageous.

To facilitate is to serve, and to serve is to
facilitate.

Stewardship is the team tenet.

明帝

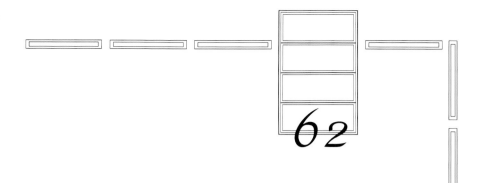

First Possess the Tao

When one adheres to the Tao, it provides.

Team leaders help others to reach their
objectives.
When team members need skill development,
team leaders provide training.
When some are deficient in knowledge,
team leaders provide information.
When some lack self-awareness,
team leaders guide them to the Tao.

Team leaders must first possess the Tao.

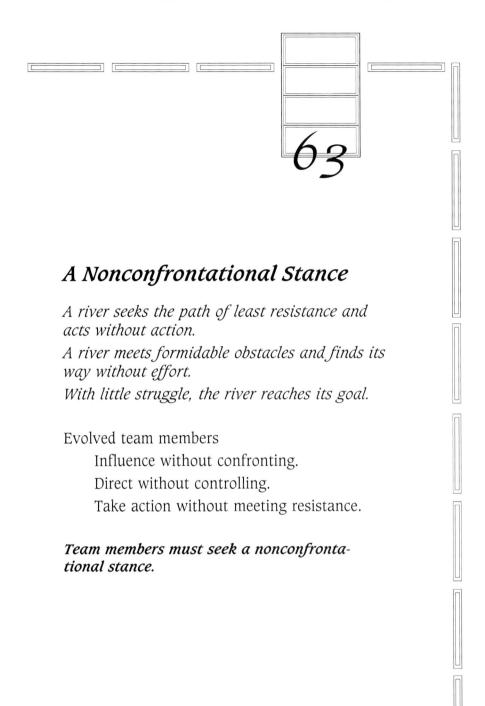

A Nonconfrontational Stance

A river seeks the path of least resistance and acts without action.

A river meets formidable obstacles and finds its way without effort.

With little struggle, the river reaches its goal.

Evolved team members

    Influence without confronting.

    Direct without controlling.

    Take action without meeting resistance.

Team members must seek a nonconfrontational stance.

開始

Guiding Events by Knowing Their Beginning

What has not begun is easy to start; what is at rest is easy to stimulate; what is just born is easy to develop.

Those who act too soon, spoil things.

Those who manipulate in the beginning, lose things.

Evolved team members

    Know instinctively when events begin.

    Manage things before they begin.

    Make order before there is disorder.

    Understand how to guide events.

    Know how to guide a situation through to completion.

Team members guide events by knowing where they begin.

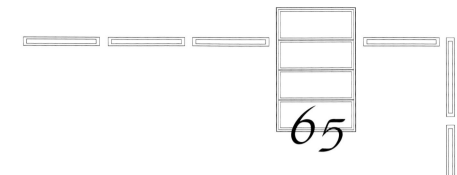

Subtlety Reflects One's Ability to Influence

Those who know the Tao are not obvious to others; they appear clever yet simple.

Those who do not know the Tao appear obvious to others and cause a reaction; they appear complex.

Those who lead with deception will cause harm to the team.

Those who lead with honest simplicity will benefit the team.

Those who know these two things understand the patterns of the Tao. This knowledge is profound.

Subtle behavior reflects a team member's ability to influence.

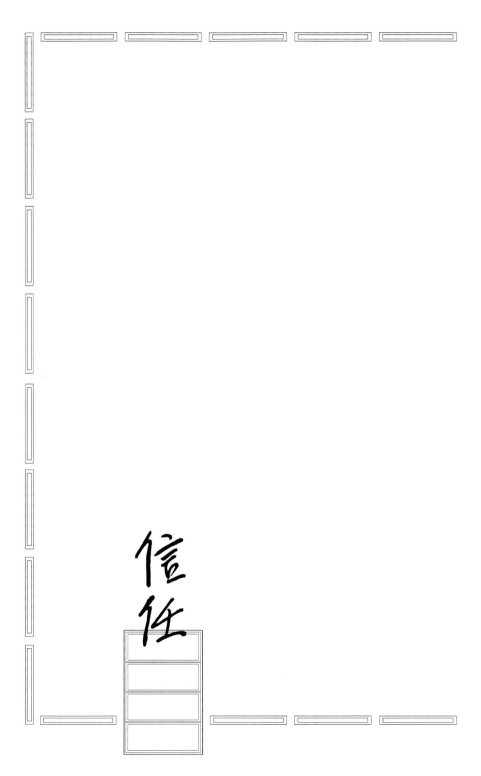

信任

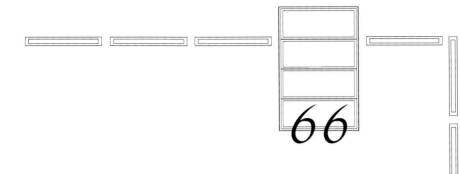

Winning the Trust of Others

*Streams and rivers pour into the sea because
the sea is lower.*
The sea has great power yet does not force itself.

When leading the team, one should never place
oneself above other team members.
Like the sea, staying low yields the greatest power.
Evolved team members
> Promote the will of others.
> Identify with others.
> Gain the support of others.

**Winning the trust of others makes a team
member more effective.**

仁
慈

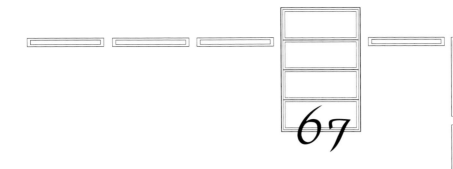

Kindness Must Be the First Virtue

The Tao's force is great. Some call it inconceivable; others call it significant.

There are those who understand the Tao, and those who do not.

For those who know the Tao, it teaches
many things, but three things stand out:
kindness, gentleness, and daring not to be last.

With kindness, one becomes noble.

With gentleness, one becomes strong.

Daring not to be last makes one first.

If one of the three is done without the others,
the action is doomed!

Kindness must be a team member's first virtue.

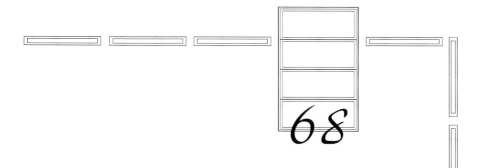

Skillful Leaders

The skillful team leader is modest.
The skillful team leader is sympathetic.
The skillful team leader shows composure.

The power in modesty and the strength in
sympathy allow team leaders to organize
and lead without being obvious.

**Skillful team leaders need not prove themselves
again and again.**

謙讓

Gaining Strength by Yielding

It is better to wait than to make the first move.

*It is better to fall back a foot than to advance
an inch.*

*This is called movement without advancement,
pushing forward through resistance.*

*Underestimating resistance escalates tension
and leads to great misfortune.*

People who initiate a move of resistance are not
centered and can be thrown easily; yet, they
must be respected.

Team members gain strength by yielding.

指點

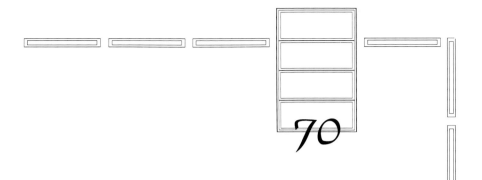

The Tao Speaks to All

My knowledge is easy to know, very easy to comprehend; yet, few are able to understand me.

The words that I speak have an origin, a beginning; yet, few are able to hear me.

The feelings I experience begin in my center; yet, few are able to empathize with me.

Since only a few understand all of these things, many do not know me.

The ones who do know me, find me in their hearts.

The Tao speaks to all team members if they are willing to listen.

不詳

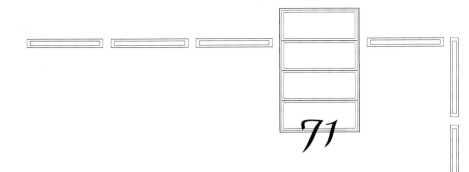

There Is Always Something That Is Unknown

To recognize that you are unhealthy is the best way to be free of the sickness.

To admit that you don't have an answer is healthy.
Presuming to know when you do not is unhealthy.

Successful team members recognize that there is always something that they do not know.

尊敬

Maintaining Appropriate Respect

When the team no longer fears authority, it signals the approach of a greater power.

Successful team members do not show disrespect to leaders; they do not reject them.

When team members show the leaders respect, the leaders return it.

Evolved team members

Minimize the distance between leaders and followers.

Focus on the give and take of authority.

Model the behaviors of their leaders.

Team members maintain appropriate respect.

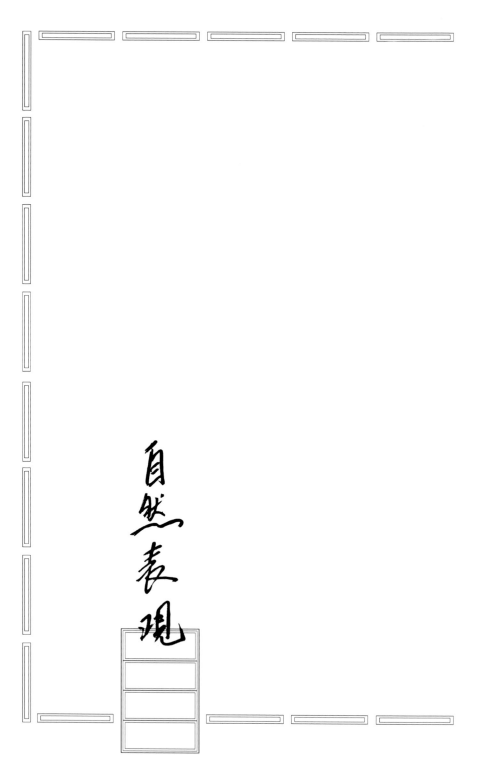

自然表現

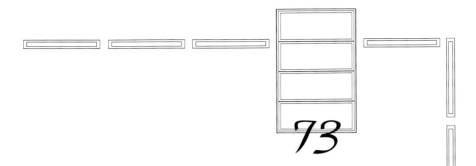

Modeling the Tao's Natural Behavior

The Tao in nature is powerful and astute.
It challenges without force.
It responds without reaction.
It is present without being called.
It organizes without direction.
The Tao's influence covers the universe.

Team members must model the Tao's
natural behavior.

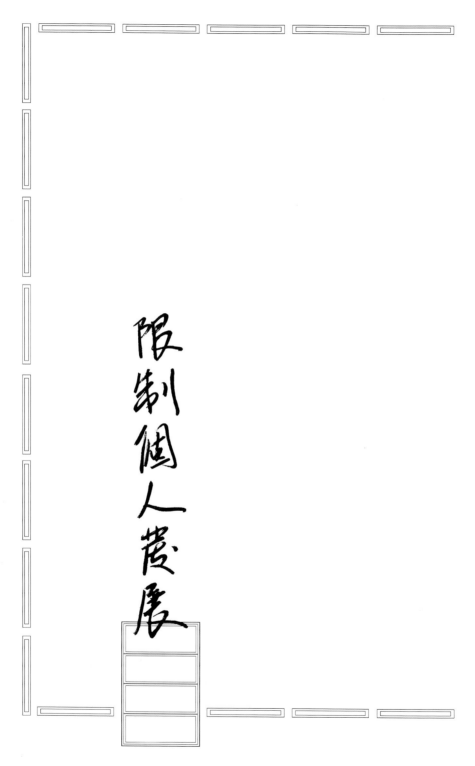

限制個人發展

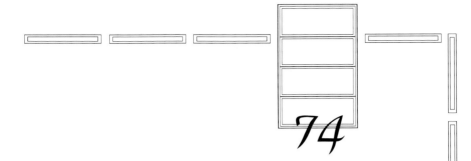

Restrictions Can Inhibit Development

When one realizes that the only constant is change, there is nothing to keep.

When one is unafraid of death, anything in the universe is possible.

When trying to control the future, one must live with a past that remains the same.

Evolved team members

> Recognize that people are good-hearted.
>
> Know that people require personal freedom.
>
> Understand that people need to be able to choose their own direction.

Restrictions must not inhibit team-member development.

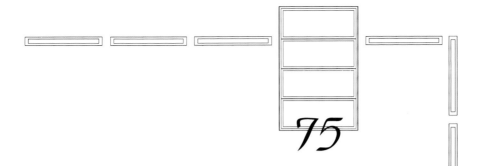

Trust

*When leaders overmanage, team members want
more autonomy and become difficult to manage.*

*When leaders want to micromanage the group,
team members ridicule those who control.*

Organizations that constantly interfere with
their teams will not endure for long.

Organizations must trust their teams.

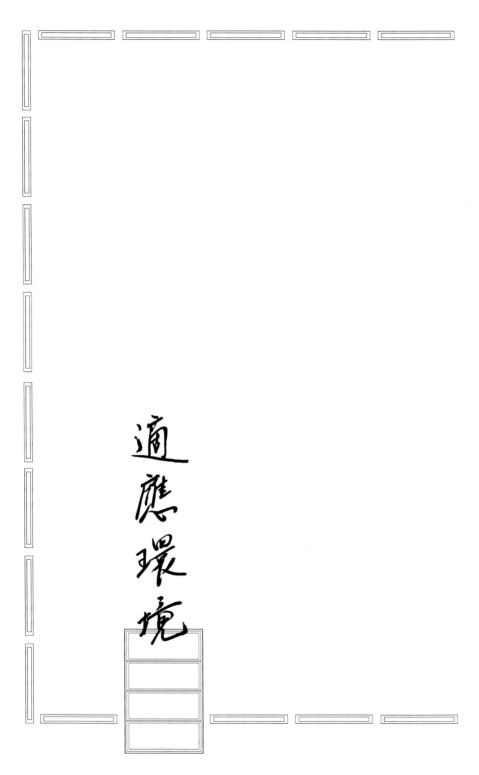

適應環境

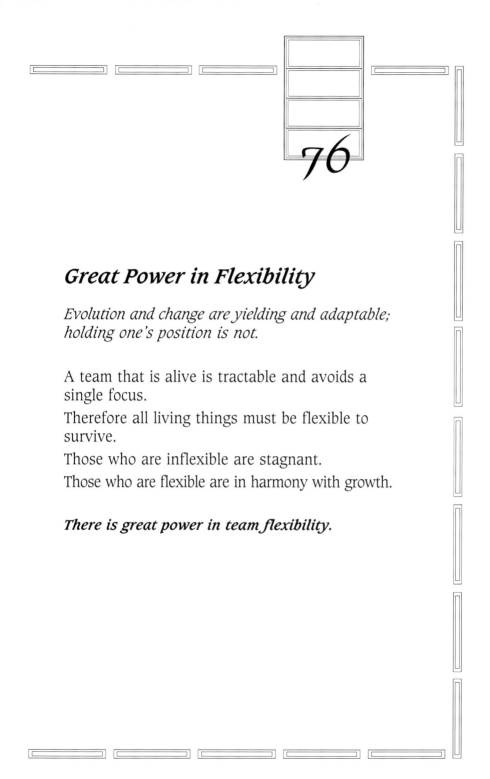

Great Power in Flexibility

Evolution and change are yielding and adaptable;
holding one's position is not.

A team that is alive is tractable and avoids a
single focus.

Therefore all living things must be flexible to
survive.

Those who are inflexible are stagnant.

Those who are flexible are in harmony with growth.

There is great power in team flexibility.

指示

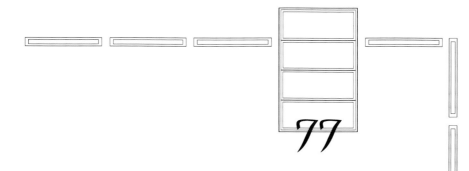

Directing the Tao's Power

In the world, the Tao acts like a bent bow.

When the bow is used, both ends bend toward the middle in perfect balance.

The bow self-adjusts for excess and deficiency.

In nature, the Tao acts like the bow.

It reduces the excess and adds to the deficit.

Those who follow the Tao understand nature's tendency to balance extremes.

Dominant species succumb to the most fragile.

Overcharged particles seek less-charged particles for balance.

Individuals who attempt to dominate are neutralized.

Who can use this information to serve others?
Those who acknowledge the Tao.

Evolved team members direct the Tao's power.

接受

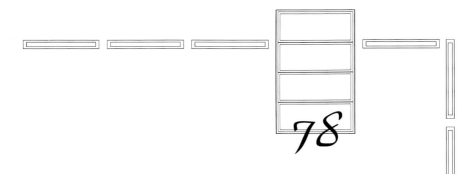

Being As Yielding and Receptive As Water

Nothing in the world is as yielding and receptive as water.

Because it has no boundaries, it can erode hard obstacles.

Nothing can surpass water's power.

In the world, pliability overcomes rigidity.

Softness overcomes hardness.

Gentleness overcomes harshness.

Thus, successful team members must be as yielding and receptive as water.

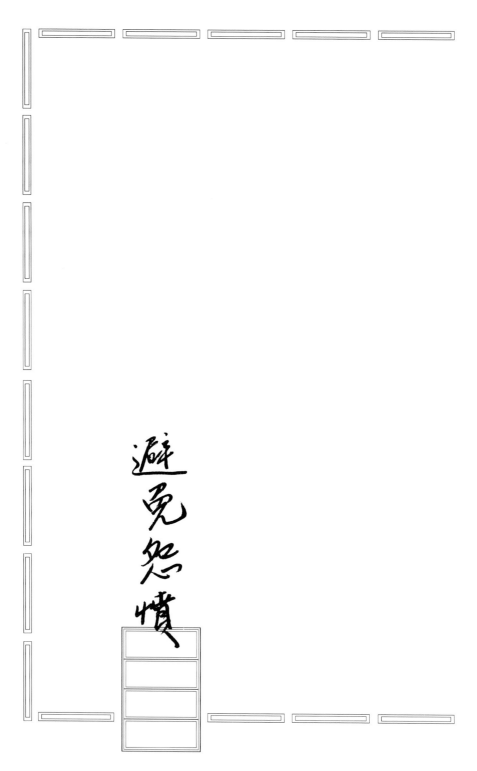

避免怨憤

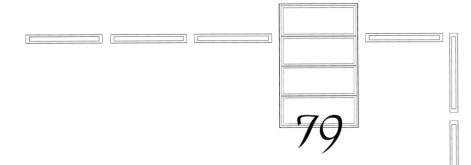

Averting Lingering Resentment

When a team member holds a strong belief,
it is difficult sometimes to compromise.

When a team member compromises but
withholds true feelings, some resentment occurs.

It is easy for resentment to linger.

Evolved team members

> Share their true feelings.
>
> Create harmony in words and deeds.
>
> Are compassionate and generous in their
> behavior toward others.

**Assume responsibility for averting lingering
resentment.**

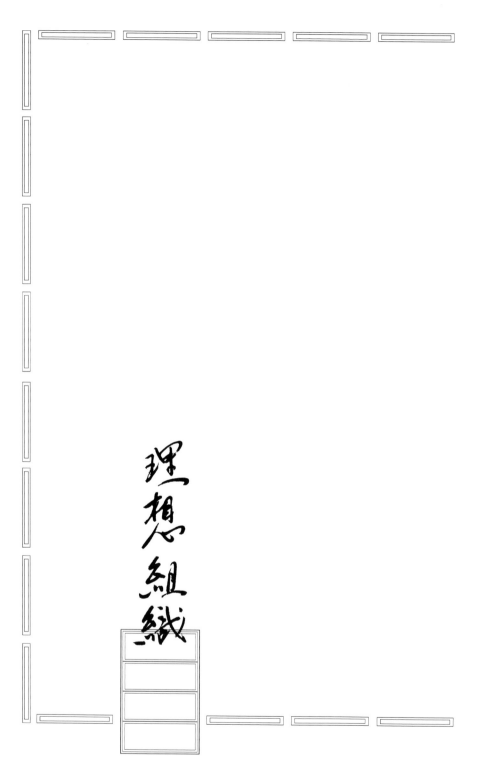

理想組織

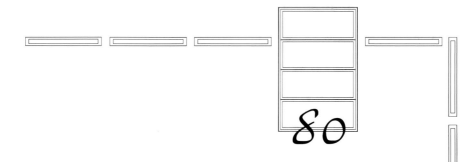

Ideal Work Systems

*If the team is led wisely, team members will
be content.*

*If the team creates a work climate where
everyone can contribute, team members
will be productive.*

*If the team provides for personal development,
team members will value the quality of their lives.*

Evolved team members

    Recognize their own potential.

    Develop a strong sense of personal power.

    Promote pride in their team.

**Recognize that successful teams are ideal
work systems.**

成功